How to Handle

DIFFICULT

PARENTS

a teacher's survival guide

Suzanne Capek Tingley

Illustrated by Judy Larson

Cottonwood Press, Inc.

COTTONWOOD PRESS INC.

109-B Cameron Drive

Fort Collins, Colorado 80525

1-800-864-4297

www.cottonwoodpress.com

Printed in the United States of America

Illustrated by Judy Larson

ISBN 978-1-877673-72-6

To my husband Larry
for his unflagging support and encouragement.

To my daughters Jennifer and Rebecca, writers also.

And to the many fine parents and dedicated teachers
with whom I've had the honor to work.

TABLE OF CONTENTS

DEALING WITH PARENTS 101

Most new teachers love working with kids. Optimists by nature, they enter the classroom ready to make a difference.

They have studied reading, math, physical education, music, English, science, special education, or social studies. They have learned how to write lesson plans and create valid tests. They have practiced effective teaching strategies and classroom management techniques during their student teaching or internship experiences. In short, they arrive at their first teaching jobs eager to embrace the challenges of the profession.

So why do so many of them leave the field within the first five years?

Teachers are unprepared to handle difficult parents. Despite all of their training, nothing really prepares teachers for working with some of today's parents.

What are they to do with Justin's mother, for example, who believes that sticking mozzarella sticks up his nose during lunch is a fine way for her son to express his individuality?

Or Samantha's stepdad, who thinks it's the teacher's fault that Samantha cheated on her social studies test?

Or Nikki's mother, who did her daughter's science project for her and then complained that it was only worth a B?

Or Bradley's father, who threatened to have the teacher fired if she didn't change his son's math grade?

Dealing with difficult parents isn't the only reason that teachers abandon the profession. However, the stress of dealing with difficult parents remains one of the top reasons teachers cite for leaving the ranks, according to the Center for the Study of Teaching and Policy (*Time*, February 21, 2005).

The stress of dealing with difficult parents remains one of the top reasons teachers cite for leaving the ranks.

Teachers need to learn parent management skills. Teachers who remain in the classroom discover that, in addition to classroom management skills, they must develop parent management skills as well. Without such skills, an adversarial relationship between a teacher and a parent can take its toll.

For example, when teachers know that a child's parent stands ready to challenge them at every turn, they can become reluctant to confront inappropriate student behavior or lack of effort. When they know that a dreaded "helicopter mom" is always hovering nearby, ready to swoop in at a moment's notice to protect her child, they may feel that it's not worth the personal hassle to stand up for what they know is in the child's best interest. When they know that a student's father will go directly to the principal if he's unhappy with his child's grade, they begin to feel perpetually defensive. In short, dealing with difficult parents can have a demoralizing effect on the individual teacher and even on the school as a whole.

Let me hasten to point out that I am not talking about the majority of parents. Most parents are supportive, helpful, and realistic. They volunteer as band boosters and help with bake sales. They attend their kids' performances and vote for the school budget. They take an interest in their child's progress, work with teachers as partners, and communicate with them respectfully and civilly. Though they sometimes disagree with the school's position, that is their right. (It's fine for parents to disagree. It's not fine for them to be disagreeable.)

Let me also point out that, yes, difficult teachers exist in every school system, creating their own set of problems. However, even the best and most reasonable teachers around the country are reporting a growing number of parents who make excuses for their children, refuse to allow them to take any responsibility, make unreasonable demands, and criticize or even threaten their children's teachers when they don't meet those demands.

Any teacher can develop an array of strategies that will prove successful a great deal of the time.

All teachers can learn to handle parents more effectively.

What can a teacher do when faced with a problem parent? No single strategy will work for all situations. However, any teacher can develop an array of strategies that will prove successful a great deal of the time. In the chapters that follow, I will describe those effective strategies and show how they can be utilized in specific situations.

A SHORT AND SUBJECTIVE
HISTORY OF PARENTS

THE ANCIENTS

In the early 1900s, Mark Twain observed that "Out of the public school grows the greatness of a nation." Others agreed. The waves of immigrants to the United States in the first quarter of the twentieth century resulted in legislation making public school attendance compulsory for children for the first time. Compulsory education not only "Americanized" the younger generation, but it also kept them out of the factories where children had previously competed with adults for jobs.

During those years and for many years that followed, parents went to work and their children went to school, the children often moving well beyond their parents in terms of formal education. Few parents questioned how the school was run or whether or not their children were being taught well or treated fairly. They believed school was their children's responsibility, just as work was theirs.

When my brother and sister and I were children in the 1950s and 1960s, for example, our parents did not contact our teachers if we didn't like an assignment. They did not call the principal to complain if we got detention. They did not believe that we never lied. They did not care if we were bored in school, and they did not accept being bored as an excuse for poor grades. They did not believe that children had "personality conflicts" with teachers because children's personalities had little standing in their book. They did not tell us that we should respect teachers only if they respected us. They were wise enough to know that our version of what happened at school that day was just that— our version. They did not know what our math homework was and they didn't care. Whatever it was, they expected us to do it.

They were not bad parents. In fact, they were great parents. They were very clear, however, about their expectations for us in terms of school. Like the parents in every other family we knew, their expectation was this: "If you get in trouble at school, that's nothing compared to what will happen when you get home."

I don't want to give the impression that my parents didn't care about us or about our education. They did. They made sure we reported to school every single day unless we were running a fever or throwing up. They knew when report cards were issued, they reviewed them, and then they signed them. They went to all our concerts, plays, and awards programs. (The only things they didn't attend were our summer baseball or softball league games. Watching us do the same thing we did in the middle of our street, except on a field where first base was a sack instead of the sewer cover, was not a reason to take off work. In truth, the only parents who ever watched us play ball in the summer were dads who were out of work for one reason or another.)

They were just busy—busy attending to their responsibilities of working hard, raising a family, paying the bills. We were expected to attend to our responsibilities—going to school every day, staying out of trouble, and paying attention. In a sense, they had their jobs and we had ours.

We did not feel deprived.

Things start to change. I became a teacher myself in the late 1970s, and it seemed to me that parents of that era were, for the most part, similar to my parents. They still expected their kids to do their job while they did theirs. They were still suspicious of their children's renditions

They did not know what our math homework was and they didn't care. Whatever it was, they expected us to do it.

of what happened in school that day, and they still expected their children to behave. Here's a typical conversation from that era:

Teacher: Tommy swore in class today.

Mr. Smith: I'm sorry. We'll take care of it at home.

Teacher: He is going to need to serve a detention.

Mr. Smith: That's fine with us.

Here's another example:

Teacher: If Madeline can stay after school on
  Thursdays, I can help her with spelling.

Mrs. Torres: She'll be there. You hear that, Madeline?
  Every Thursday.

However, by the early eighties, I began to see a slight abdication of parental authority. Typical conversations of that era tended to sound more like this:

Teacher: Mrs. Jones, I'm having a little trouble getting
  Jack to do his homework.

Mrs. Jones: If you can't make him do it, what do you
  expect me to do?

Or:

Teacher: Mr. Fazio, Jennifer really needs to stay after
  school for extra help.

Mr. Fazio: Well, she's a lot like me—doesn't like to be
  told what to do.

Around this time we began to hear about "bored" children. Kids who had formerly been described as "lazy" (a word we teachers were now forbidden to use) were now "bored." Reading bored them. Math bored them. Writing bored them. Homework especially bored them.

Kids who had formerly been described as "lazy" (a word we teachers were now forbidden to use) were now "bored."

The reason for all this boredom? These kids were *way* smarter than the other kids, according to their parents.

Of course, these students typically didn't demonstrate their boredom by staring out the window, doodling, or coming up with creative solutions for problems. Instead, they did no work at all or disrupted the class. This, according to their parents, was because they weren't being sufficiently challenged.

No one I knew when I was a kid ever admitted to being bored. I learned early in life never to say to my mother, "There's nothing to do around here," because she would quickly find something for me to do: vacuum, pick beans, take out the garbage, clean the garage. It never would have occurred to her (or to me) that it was her job to entertain me if I were bored.

I began to feel that was exactly what some parents expected me to do with their kids—entertain them.

However, as a teacher, I began to feel that was exactly what some parents expected me to do with their kids—entertain them. If their children weren't doing anything in class, it wasn't because they were lazy or because they had legitimate problems like learning disabilities. It was because they were so smart that the work in class was beneath them. The "challenge" they needed was really mine: to entertain them.

By this point, I had kids of my own. Watching *Sesame Street* with them, I began to see how they could grow up believing that

all learning could be fun. Number facts should be set to music, and letters could sing and dance!

Well, I wanted learning to be fun, too, but I knew that was not always possible. Although my 1980s hair style made me look like one, I was not a Muppet.

The decade ends. Toward the end of the 1980s, I began to see a big difference in the attitude of some parents toward schools, toward teachers, and toward their own kids. By then, I had become the principal of a middle school/high school, and many conversations with parents began to sound like this:

Principal: Mr. Yung, Jeremy was in a fight this afternoon
and I am going to have to suspend him for a day.

Mr. Yung: What about the other kid? He started it! He
better be getting two days!

Or:

Principal: Mrs. Golden, Ann was disrespectful to her
physical education teacher this afternoon.

Mrs. Golden: How was she disrespectful?

Principal: She told the teacher that she wasn't going to
do any f-ing push-ups.

Mrs. Golden: So what did her teacher do to provoke her?

Unfortunately, this trend continued over the next years, headed steadily, in my opinion, downhill. Today when a student has a problem at school, there's a much greater chance that the parents will not accept the consequences of their child's behavior without argument.

When a child gets in trouble today, conversations are more likely to sound like the one I had not long ago over an incident involving a middle schooler:

Today when a student has a problem in school, there's a much greater chance that the parents will not accept the consequences of their child's behavior without argument.

Principal: Mike, whatever made you think that mooning
the other team from the bus was a good idea?

Mike: *(Shrugging his shoulders)* I dunno.

As a middle schooler, Mike probably *didn't* know. (It's a given that middle schoolers sometimes don't think before they act.) But when told Mike was being suspended for a few days to ponder the question, his father gave this response:

Mike's dad: You're overreacting. Didn't you ever do
something like that?

I wondered briefly what there is about me that would make Mike's dad think that I too mooned an opposing team when I was 13.

However, here's what I said to him:

Principal: Oh, for Pete's sake. Gimme a break. No wonder your kid thinks mooning someone is okay.

All right. I didn't say that, of course. I *thought* it, though. Here's what I really said:

Principal: Mike may return to school in three days.

There have always been demanding parents. However, demanding parents of earlier times were more likely to demand that their *kids* do what they wanted them to do, not the *teachers*.

*What best
describes
parents today?
In my opinion,
it is a belief
that their kids
should have
anything their
little hearts
desire.*

THE MODERNS

What best describes parents today? In my opinion, it is a belief that their kids should have anything their little hearts desire. Unfortunately, schools may have contributed to this notion. That wasn't the intent, of course, but the result of a good idea run amok.

Starting in schools in the early 1980s and continuing into this century was a belief in the importance of self-esteem. It was deemed more important than reading and math, more important than discipline, more important than problem solving, more important than just about anything. At its worst, though no one actually said it, it took the form of, "Well, if little Mikey can't read, at least he can feel good about himself as an illiterate."

Competition became inherently bad because if someone were first, someone else would have to be last. The baseballs and the double dutch jump ropes were put in the closet, and instead we played cooperative games like grasping the edges of a silk parachute and watching the wind lift it up.

All too often, everyone got a ribbon just for participating. Perfect attendance awards were given out for near-perfect attendance as well (absent fewer than 15 times!). Ten kids in a class received the "Most Improved" award at the end of the year. "Inventive" spelling sometimes lasted far beyond elementary school and didn't need to be corrected before the written piece was displayed on the bulletin board. The "math minute" became the "math six minutes" so that no one would feel bad about not finishing the ten problems required for a star.

Mr. Rogers liked us all just the way we were, and Barney loved us, sight unseen. Everyone was special in his or her own way. There were no "wrong" answers. Conversations often went something like this:

> **Teacher:** How much is 6 times 8?
> **Student:** 36?
> **Teacher:** Good try! What else could it be?

Competition became inherently bad because if someone were first, someone else would have to be last.

Remembered to bring pencil to class

1st Place

Grades of A, B, and C on elementary report cards often changed to new, inoffensive letters that carried no baggage—like "N" (needs improvement), "M" (making progress), and "S" (sometimes gets it).

All right, I'm exaggerating, but there was a tendency to believe that raising self-esteem required lowering our expectations. We began to believe that children should be rewarded not only for doing something good, but also for not doing something bad:

Teacher: Because no one hit anyone today, tomorrow we
will have a popcorn party!

Raising a child's self-esteem also meant asking rather than telling children what we wanted them to do.

Raising a child's self-esteem also meant *asking* rather than *telling* children what we wanted them to do. Teachers needed to give children choices.

Old way: Class, get out your spelling books.
New way: Class, would you like to work on spelling now?

Or:

Old way: If you can't share, we'll put those toys away. And stop that pinching immediately or you'll find yourself in the time-out chair!
New way: We need you to share those toys, okay? And no more pinching, all right?

Or:

Old way: Put the balls away now.
New way: We need to put the balls away now, okay? Is everybody ready to put the balls away? Okay, let's put them all away, all right?

Of course, children were smart enough to sense that putting the balls away or not was not a real choice like, "Do you want mustard on your hot dog?" or "Do you want to go swimming or go to the mall?" They knew instinctively that responding with a resounding "No!" to "Is everybody ready to put the balls away?" would simply result in more wheedling from the adult. Though they knew that play time would eventually end, they also knew they didn't have to do what was asked the first time or maybe even the fifth or sixth time. They would be able to tell when the teacher actually meant what she said because then she would go back to the old way of giving directions:

Teacher: "Put those balls away NOW!"

Self-esteem isn't raised by lowering expectations. All of this is not to say that self-esteem doesn't matter. It does. No one should have to be picked last in a gym class. There are dozens of ways of choosing up sides without making a kid feel like a loser before the game even gets started. And there are hundreds of ways, maybe thousands of ways, maybe millions of ways of helping kids grow, learn, and make good mistakes on their way to discovering how to make good decisions.

The problem is that in our eagerness to help kids feel good about themselves, we unwittingly overlooked the one thing guaranteed to achieve that result: actual accomplishment. Even a kindergartner knows when he's done something really worthy of praise. In our rush to enhance self-esteem, we simply underestimated how important real accomplishment is to kids.

Kids want to do well, and they want to please. They want to know what the target is so they can try to hit it. They also want consistent adult guidance and direction as they learn how to do things.

With the emphasis on self-esteem, teachers often soft pedaled criticism and lowered their standards in a misguided attempt not to harm the child's delicate psyche. Kids discovered to their initial delight and later dismay that even their smallest efforts were

Even a kindergartner knows when he's done something really worthy of praise.

rewarded. All those trophies and certificates really didn't mean anything if everyone got them. (Have you ever noticed at elementary awards ceremonies, where everyone gets a certificate of some kind, that many kids leave their awards on the floor under their chairs when the ceremony is over?) So, being kids, they began to test the limits to see how far they had to go before an adult would actually step up to the plate.

All those trophies and certificates really didn't mean anything if everyone got them.

Parents join the self-esteem movement. Taking their lead from school, parents also began to believe that a child's self-esteem could be damaged easily if any of his or her actions or ideas met with disapproval. For far too many parents, the word "no" became both rare and negotiable.

Parents momentarily forgot who was in charge:

Mom: *(to her five-year-old)* Mommy's tired of the escalator. Aren't you tired of the escalator? Okay, one more time. But then we need to go home, okay? Well, just one more time after that. Then that's it, okay?

Parents forgot that actions speak louder than words:

Parent: Johnny, don't make me come over there. Johnny, I mean it. Don't make me come over there. Stop that now. I don't want to have to come over there. You hear me? I mean it. Don't make me come over there.

Parents forgot that they were older and more experienced than their kids:

Dad: *(to his nine-year old)* How many times do I have to tell you not to pee on the rhododendrons? Look! They're all dead. I've told you a dozen times. How long are you going to keep doing that?!

And some parents seemed to have momentarily lost their minds:

Mom: *(to her toddler, at the the grocery store)* I know you're angry and you can hit Mommy, but not too hard.

One result of the self-esteem movement was that kids' self-esteem stayed the same but adults' self-esteem plummeted. Kids began to believe that if nothing was actually required of them, they must be entitled to do whatever they wanted. For a while there it wasn't pretty.

Eventually, however, most teachers and parents got tired of asking kids a dozen times to do what they were supposed to do. When many of them came to their senses, they began to remember that when a child misbehaves, it doesn't necessarily signal a lack of confidence, but instead a lack of discipline. Or maybe a lack of clear expectations on the part of the adult. Or maybe (gasp!) a lack of consequences.

Today the operative concept in education isn't self-esteem, but assessment— a test for everything.

The pendulum swings. Of course, keeping with education tradition, schools didn't just recognize the error of their ways. They overcompensated. The pendulum swung *w-a-a-ay* to the other side. Today the operative concept in education isn't self-esteem, but *assessment*—a test for everything.

*When teachers
and parents
work together,
the child
benefits.*

Not long ago kids got ribbons just for running around the soccer field in the summer or remembering their lunch money for a week or learning their five weekly vocabulary words. Now we test them in every class, at every level, in every subject. Kids can forget about ribbons for participation. Either they can pass the test or they can't.

What happens to a child's self-esteem when a low test score lands her in third grade for a second time? Or when a ten-year-old with the ability of a preschooler is forced, because the state mandates it, to sit for a two hour test? Or when a high school student with superior computer programming skills can't pass the required foreign language test? Self-esteem is no longer the major concern. Test scores are.

Wouldn't a little moderation be nice for a change?

High stakes testing makes parents nervous for their children, and rightfully so. All parents want their children to be successful, and not just so Dad's car can sport a bumper sticker proclaiming, "My child is on the Supreme Deluxe Honor Roll," as if his kid were some kind of taco. Parents want their children to have friends, to get good grades, and to like school. It may not always seem that way to the teacher, but parents really do want their children to have a positive attitude toward teachers and toward learning.

There are variables in education and there are constants. One thing that hasn't changed in all the history of parents is that kids do better when there is mutual support and respect between home and school. Hot button issues in education come and go, but a strong connection between home and school remains one of the most reliable indicators of a child's potential for success. In developing strategies to work with parents, it is crucial that teachers never forget this important idea—that when teachers and parents work together, the child benefits.

THE ACORN MAY NOT FALL
FAR FROM THE OAK

After school has been in session for a few weeks, most teachers have identified some concerns they have about some of their students. Of course, a natural course of action is to meet with each set of parents to see if they can share any insight into working with their child. But what if, five minutes into a parent-teacher conference, you find yourself with a clarity you didn't expect?

Imagine the following conversation, for example:

Teacher: Heidi is a smart girl, but when I ask her to stop talking, she gives me attitude.

Parent: *(big sigh)* Like what?

Teacher: She's disrespectful.

Parent: How is she disrespectful?

Teacher: The expression on her face and her tone of voice.

Parent: *(rolling her eyes)* Oh, big deal.

Or:

Teacher: Tim needs to clean up his language.

Parent: Sh-t, he's just a kid.

Or:

Parent: This is the third time this year you've sent Bart
home with head lice.

School Nurse: He can't be in school with nits.

Parent: He looked pretty good this morning.

School Nurse: Did you check his head?

Parent: No, but he looked in the mirror and said they
were gone.

Or:

Teacher: The problem is that when I try to correct
Annie's behavior, she insists that she's not doing
anything wrong.

Parent: Maybe she isn't.

Teacher: I've watched her break another student's
crayons and then deny doing it.

Parent: Are you sure it was Annie?

Or:

Teacher: Misha has a hard time sitting still. She seems
to have trouble focusing or staying on task.

Parent: Uh huh. So when did you say the field trip was?

Or:

Teacher: Patrick has a problem with telling the truth.

Parent: I've never seen that at home.

Or:

Principal: I'm suspending Logan for fighting.

Parent: *(slamming her hand on table)* Listen! I've told all my
kids—if someone hits you, you hit 'em back!

*While you may
understand a
child better
after meeting
his or her
parents, that
fact alone will
not ensure a
good working
relationship
between parent
and teacher.*

Or:

Parent: My son got a ticket for parking in front of the gym!

Coach: He parked in a handicapped space.

Parent: He was late for practice.

Coach: He's not handicapped.

Parent: I think the laws discriminate against able-bodied persons. Just because he doesn't have a handicap, he's excluded from certain parking places. It's not fair!

While you may understand a child better after meeting his or her parents, that fact alone will not ensure a good working relationship between parent and teacher. It may help you to gauge the extent of the challenge, however!

Like their offspring, all parents are different. Just as good teachers must develop skills to work with all kinds of students, they must also develop skills to work with all kinds of parents.

Even though individual parents are different, anyone who has worked with students and their parents for a few years can't help but notice that certain attitudes and points of view appear again and again. The names and faces change, but their expectations remain the same.

In the following chapters we're going to look at some recurring types of parental behaviors that can make your life as a teacher miserable unless you are prepared to respond to them with confidence. If you have thought about how to handle unreasonable demands—what to say and how to say it—encounters with demanding parents can be less unnerving. Preparation will increase your chances of success.

You might take the advice of a golf coach to his players: "Think about your play and walk like you mean it."

Just as good teachers must develop skills to work with all kinds of students, they must also develop skills to work with all kinds of parents.

PINOCCHIO'S MOM

Despite abundant evidence to the contrary, Pinocchio's Mom insists that her child doesn't lie. It is hard to tell whether she actually believes this or is foolish enough to think that others will actually believe it. She makes a teacher want to jump up and scream, "Liar, liar, pants on fire!"

There are more professional ways of handling this, however.

Pinocchio (or Pinocchia) is usually well aware that his mother will believe whatever he says. He is also often smart enough to take advantage of her readiness to defend him. If he gets in trouble in school, he understands that his best course of action is to get to his mother before the teacher does and spin his version of what happened.

Mom: *(on phone)* Pinocchio came home today and said that a boy in his class tripped him on the playground. He says you saw it and didn't do anything about it. He has a red mark on his forehead.

Teacher: That's not exactly what happened.

Mom: Pinocchio said the boy hit him, too. And you didn't do anything about it.

Teacher: As I said, that's not exactly what happened.

Mom: Are you calling my son a liar?

Teacher: I'm not calling anyone a liar. But what happened was that Pinocchio pushed Anthony off the swing.

Mom: That's not what Pinocchio said. And I know my son doesn't lie.

We all know where this is going—around and around and around. Pinocchio's Mom would much rather focus on what the teacher did or didn't do than on what her child did or didn't do. The teacher needs to help the parent refocus on the child's behavior.

Pinocchio's Mom would much rather focus on what the teacher did or didn't do than on what her child did or didn't do.

Mom: Pinocchio came home today and said that a boy in his class tripped him on the playground. He says you saw it and didn't do anything about it. He has a red mark on his forehead.

Teacher: Well, we all know what a little liar your son is.

Ha ha! Just a little joke there. The teacher may *want* to say that, but of course she wouldn't unless she plans on leaving at the end of the year. Or sooner.

Here's another possibility:

Mom: Pinocchio came home today and said that a boy in his class tripped him on the playground. He says you saw it and didn't do anything about it. He has a red mark on his forehead.

Teacher: Yup, that's me. I let them do whatever they want.

Gotcha again! Remember that the first rule when dealing with irate parents is, "No sarcasm!" (It should also be parents' first rule in dealing with teachers, of course.) Got that? No sarcasm!

Here's a more productive way of handling the conversation:

Mom: Pinocchio came home today and said that a boy in his class tripped him on the playground. He says

you saw it and didn't do anything about it. He has a
red mark on his forehead.

Teacher: Did he give you any more specifics?

Mom: No, just that the boy tripped him.

Teacher: Did he say which boy?

Mom: *(shouting to Pinocchio)* Pin! She wants to know
which kid tripped you...*(to the teacher)*...Anthony. He
says a kid named Anthony tripped him.

Teacher: And when was this?

Mom: After lunch. Today.

Teacher: And he says I saw it?

Mom: Yes. And you didn't do anything.

Teacher: Did he tell you where on the playground this
happened?

Mom: *(to Pinocchio)* She wants to know where it happened. *(to the teacher.)* He doesn't remember.

Teacher: Well, we had a small incident on the playground today when Pinocchio pushed Anthony off
the swing. I did see that.

Mom: *(a little doubtful)* That's not the way he tells it.

Teacher: Well, you may want to ask him about that. And
I'll be happy to talk to him about his story tomorrow.

*Refuse to be
sucked into a
debate about
who is telling
the truth.*

Focus on specifics: who, what, when, where, and how. Even the
most gullible parent does not want to be made to look like a fool.
Refuse to be sucked into a debate about who is telling the truth. It
isn't about who's lying, the teacher or the student, but what actually
happened.

Let's try another example:

Parent: Pinocchia says you gave her a zero for her
research paper.

Teacher: She didn't hand anything in.

Parent: Pinocchia says she left it on your desk when
you were out of the room.

Teacher: I didn't find a paper on my desk.

Parent: Are you saying my daughter is lying?

Okay, what's the teacher's next response?

a) Yup, like a rug.

*Also keep
in the back of
your mind that,
despite evidence
to the contrary,
you could be
wrong.*

b) Look at her nose!

c) When exactly did she say she left it on my desk?

You're right. *Think* the first two, but *say* the third. Also keep in
the back of your mind that, despite evidence to the contrary, you
could be wrong. Try to keep an open mind and follow up with questions like these:

- What was the title of her paper?
- Did it have a cover?
- Why didn't she hand it in when I collected the rest
  of the papers?
- Why didn't she mention to me that she left the
  paper on my desk?

If this is the first time Pinocchia has tried this trick, or if there is
even the slightest possibility in your own mind that she could be telling
the truth, you will probably end up accepting a late paper. Raise
enough questions, though, that there is significant doubt in the parent's mind that Pinocchia actually did what she claimed she did. You
also need to make it clear that this is a one-time ploy for Pinocchia.
Use the magnanimous approach:

Teacher: I suppose it's possible that a paper could have
been left in the room, but I just don't know how

that could have happened. However, what I will do is allow Pinocchia until Friday to turn in another copy.

Some teachers may think that this response is caving in and "letting the kid get away with it." Well, maybe. But it's important to keep your eye on the prize: Pinocchia still has to do the assignment. She also knows not to try this trick with you again.

In my experience, there is a greater likelihood of a positive outcome in conversations with Pinocchia's mom if the student is present. If she is, I recommend that you talk directly to the student. I have a theory that it's easier for a student to lie to her mother than to you.

Pinocchia's Mom: My daughter said you wouldn't help her after school.

Teacher: *(directly to student)* I said I wouldn't help you?

Pinocchia: You said you didn't have time.

Teacher: *(to the student)* When was that?

Pinocchia: Last Tuesday.

Teacher: Oh, I remember. I told you we had a faculty meeting.

Pinocchia: *(silence)*

Teacher: Do you remember I said I'd help you the next day?

Pinocchia: No.

Teacher: You don't remember that I said to come by on Wednesday?

Pinocchia: *(silence)*

Teacher: *(to the parent)* I always offer extra help sessions on Wednesdays.

Mom: Pinocchia, is that right? Were you supposed to go on Wednesday?

Pinocchia: Maybe...

On occasion, Pinocchia will have already gotten herself in so deep with her mother that there is no way she can retreat. Kids often start out with a small lie and then for one reason or another—most likely just poor judgment—dig themselves a hole and can't find a way out.

> **Mom:** Pinocchia said she didn't know she was failing.
> **Teacher:** *(to Pinocchia)* You and I talked about this last week.
> **Pinocchia:** You didn't say I was failing.
> **Teacher:** I told you that you had a 52 average.
> **Pinocchia:** But you didn't say I was failing.
> **Mom:** I just think that you weren't very clear to Pinocchia.

Kids often start out with a small lie and then dig themselves a hole and can't find a way out.

At this point the teacher will want to say, "What do you think 52 means? That you're on the honor roll?" Instead, she will understand that Pinocchia is in over her, ah, nose.

> **Teacher:** Well, then let's be clear now. You're failing math because you don't do your homework. You're a smart girl, but you don't do the work.
> **Mom:** Pinocchia, is that right? You're not doing the work?
> **Pinocchia:** Well, I do some of it.
> **Teacher:** Some of it isn't good enough. You need to do all of it. Now, how about coming in after school on Wednesday?
> **Mom:** She'll be there.

With younger children, it still helps if the child is present, but you have to be careful not to look like a bully:

> **Mom:** Pinocchio says you said he cheated on the spelling test. Pinocchio would never cheat.

Teacher: Pinocchio, tell your mother what happened
   on the test.

Pinocchio: I already told her.

Mom: He said he was just asking for a tissue.

Teacher: Is that right? Is that what happened?

Mom: He has allergies.

Teacher: There are tissues on my desk. Pinocchio, you
   know that, right?

Pinocchio: *(He nods.)*

Teacher: So you don't have to ask anyone for anything
   during a test, right?

Pinocchio: *(He nods.)*

Teacher: So how about if you study and we take the test
   again tomorrow?

Mom: It doesn't seem fair, but okay.

*Sometimes teachers
make the mistake
of believing that
they have to get a
complete confession
out of a student.*

This technique is something I call, "Delivering the message."
Sometimes teachers make the mistake of believing that they have to
get a complete confession out of a student. They seem to think it's
not over until Pinocchio screams, "Okay! Okay! You got me, copper!
I lied! I cheated!" Then he's cuffed and led away.

There's no need for all this drama nor for students to be completely humiliated when they make the kinds of mistakes all
youngsters make. (Of course, I'm talking here of errors in youthful
judgment, not the serious kinds of mistakes that end up with kids
being suspended from school, or worse.) When you focus on delivering the message, all you need is acknowledgment that the message
has been received. For example, in the previous conversation
Pinocchio tacitly admitted his error with a nod, and the teacher let
go. She avoided putting the child in a place where he had no choice
but to continue to lie to save face.

Here's another example:

Mom: Pinocchia said she didn't know the project was
due Friday.

Teacher: Pinocchia, were you here on Monday?

Pinocchia: Yeah.

Teacher: That's the day I went over the assignment.

Pinocchia: I don't remember.

Mom: Five days doesn't seem like a very long time for
the assignment.

Teacher: Well, I have to tell you that most students got
it done.

Pinocchia: I didn't hear you.

Teacher: So what do you need to get the project finished?

*Watch for
signs that
the parent
or student
is allowing
your point.*

Watch for signs that the parent or student is allowing your point.
When Pinocchia says, "I didn't hear you," in the previous example,
the teacher moves on to resolution. Pinocchia doesn't dispute what
the teacher says, and, in actuality, subtly accepts some of the blame.
The teacher doesn't have to add, "As usual, you weren't paying attention," or, "Everyone else seemed to hear it," or, "Maybe you were
talking instead of listening," or any of the other things that teachers
have been saying to kids for a hundred years or so, with the same dull
effect. None of those observations will help and will only push
Pinocchia and her mother further away.

The teacher simply makes sure her message is delivered and
understood: "The assignment was clear and you, Pinocchia, didn't do
it." There is a much greater chance of amicable resolution to a problem if the teacher can recognize when the message has been received
and leave it at that. Remember, you should be looking for changes in
behavior, not punitive damages.

Of course, there are serious situations that do require the student to admit to wrongdoing—fighting, bullying, harassment, etc. Delivering the message is a technique for garden variety misunderstandings. However, any time a student's lie impugns your professionalism, ethics, intelligence or morals, you have the obligation and the right to defend yourself.

One other thing: You only deliver the message once. If a student does the same thing a second time, all bets are off.

> **Mom:** *(a month later)* Pinocchia didn't know that the test was Friday.
>
> Teacher: Pinocchia, how did it happen that you didn't know?
>
> **Pinocchia:** I don't know. I just didn't.
>
> **Teacher:** I announced it in class and it was written on the board.
>
> **Pinocchia:** I didn't see it.
>
> **Mom:** Is there some way she can retake the test?
>
> **Teacher:** I'm sorry. She will have other opportunities to improve her grade. As you know, we've dealt with this issue before. Pinocchia needs to write down her assignments. Maybe you could check at home to see if she does that.

Here are a few points to keep in mind when dealing with Pinocchio's Mom:

- Keep focused on specifics: who, what, when, where, how. Don't allow charges to go unquestioned.

- Have your own data clear and handy. If it's a problem of assignments not being completed, know what was assigned and when. If it's a question of a grade, have ready the rubric you used or a copy of the test. While there are times when a teacher can be completely caught off guard by a parental complaint, most teachers have a pretty good idea of what an issue is going to be when a concerned parent calls.

- If the student is present, talk to him or her directly in front of the parent. The older the student, the more direct you can be. With young children, it doesn't take much for the teacher to look like a bully. With older students, you can exert a little more pressure, but you'll want to be sure that your goal is fact-finding, not defending yourself.

Refuse to be sucked in to a confrontation over the child's truthfulness.

- Refuse to be sucked in to a confrontation over the child's truthfulness. If the parent asks an inflammatory question like, "Are you calling my child a liar?", ignore the challenge. Instead, focus your response on the issue: "We're trying to find out what exactly happened here."

- Remember that you can "deliver the message" without getting a full confession and still get the results you want.

Pinocchio's mom will rarely admit that her child, like most, sometimes lies. She doesn't know that for kids it's a survival skill, not necessarily a character flaw at this point. Nearly all of them will grow out of it.

Those who don't will have bright political futures.

CAPED CRUSADER

All parents have the right and responsibility to know what their children are learning. The Caped Crusader, however, believes his ideas or principles should be embraced by everyone. He is more than willing to fight for his ideas so that they can be applied throughout the school district.

A frequent target for the Crusader is the school curriculum. It is important to recognize that the Crusader may honestly disagree with a book choice a teacher makes and may legitimately protest having his child read it. In fact, he may have the right to *insist* that his child not read a particular book. What he doesn't have, however, is the right to choose for all the other students in the class.

A typical conversation with the Crusader goes something like this:

Crusader: We have a problem with the book you're making the class read.

Teacher: Really? What kind of problem?

Crusader: We think it's not appropriate for children to read.

Teacher: Why is that?

Crusader: Well, the language, for one thing. And what happens in the book.

Teacher: Have you read the book?

Crusader: I didn't have to. I know what it says. And I
know I speak for a lot of parents who aren't happy
about your choice but just don't have the courage to
say anything.

Teacher: No one's ever complained before.

Crusader: Like I said, people are afraid. I'm concerned
not just for my child, but for everyone's child.
Nobody should be subjected to a book like this.

*The Crusader
often likes
to imply that
he speaks for
many, many
others, so it's
important to
clarify whom
he actually
represents,
right from
the beginning.*

For some beleaguered teachers, the thought that they might be
striking fear in the heart of anyone, especially parents, seems a
stretch. They might be tempted to ask, "Just what, exactly, are these
people afraid of?" The response, however, would probably be, "They
are afraid to say."

A teacher might be inclined to ignore the Crusader as just another
wingnut complaining about a book he hasn't even read. That would
be a mistake. Annoying as it might be, he may be a test case for other
parents who are not happy with a particular book choice and who
may, in fact, become a critical mass if the issue isn't resolved to his
satisfaction.

The Crusader often likes to imply that he speaks for many, many
others, so it's important to clarify whom he actually represents, right
from the beginning.

Crusader: We have a problem with the book you're
making the class read.

Teacher: I'm not sure who "we" is. Can you clarify?

Crusader: Well, I have a problem. And my wife.

Teacher: Oh, I see. You and your wife are unhappy
with our book choice. What is your concern?

Crusader: Well, the language, for one thing.

Teacher: It's true that there are words in this book that
we ordinarily wouldn't use in the classroom.

Crusader: So why are you making the students read them?

Teacher: It is my feeling that the topic of the book—a
young man who manages to overcome great obstacles—
could be helpful to many students.

Crusader: Well, I don't want Jane reading this stuff.

Teacher: No problem. I can find an alternate book for
her.

It is important to limit the conversation to the parents at hand.
Here's another way this conversation might go:

Crusader: We have a problem with the book you're
making the class read.

Teacher: I'm not sure who "we" is.

Crusader: Well, I have a problem and so does my wife.
And so do most of the members of my church.

Teacher: Well, let's start with the concerns that you
and your wife have.

If a teacher plans to have students read a book that might be
seen by some as controversial, it is a good idea to send a letter home
to parents before students begin reading the book. The letter might
say something like this:

Dear Parents:

Next semester we are going to read Chris
Crutcher's *Whale Talk*. This book contains some
mature language, but it is part of our study of personal courage. It is the story of how a group of high
school students who see themselves as social misfits,
manage to accomplish a goal that changes their lives.

*It is important
to limit the
conversation
to the parents
at hand.*

If you would prefer your child not read this
book, please let me know and I will assign him/her
an alternate choice.

By pointing out the mature language ahead of time, a teacher
gives parents an opportunity to opt out without confrontation.
Sometimes that will head off any problem. Other times it will not.

Parents do have a right to review what their child reads and to
question a teacher's choices. They do have the right to speak for
themselves and their child. They do not have the right to speak for
everyone else and their children. To deal with parents who want to
control everyone, most school districts have a policy on censorship in
place. All teachers and librarians should know exactly what that policy says in case they have to remind their principal. Most policies
spell out the process by which a book can be challenged. Many begin
with a questionnaire that requires that the parent identify specifically
his or her objections to the book—something that cannot be accom-
plished if he hasn't read it.

If your school does not have a policy on censorship, I strongly
recommend that you talk to your principal or librarian about developing one. Some schools put together a task force composed of
teachers, library media specialists, administrators, and parents to
examine policies on censorship and make recommendations to the
school board. Sample policies can be obtained from organizations
such as the American Association of School Librarians and the
National Council of Teachers of English. You can also ask other local
school districts for copies of their policies.

But what if your school doesn't have a policy in place and your
principal doesn't want one? What if he or she prefers—in a worst case
scenario—to be the lone arbitrator on a book by book basis? If that is the
case, you will want to make sure that you keep your principal apprised

*Parents do
have a right
to review what
their child reads
and to question
a teacher's
choices.*

of your reading list and your CD/video list well in advance of classroom use. While doing so risks preemptive censorship, you absolutely do not want to go it alone without administrative support if a parent seriously objects to one of your choices. These kinds of conflicts can quickly escalate, and you do not want to have to appear at a board of education meeting trying to explain your curriculum choices in front of a hostile crowd. If you find yourself in an intolerable situation that seriously compromises your academic freedom, it's better to look for another job than to try to defend yourself without district support.

Sometimes—because of a community's values or the lack of courage on the part of an administrator—a censorship policy is ignored and a book is removed from the library shelves or from a teacher's reading list. If it happens to you, you may be forced to choose another book—or choose another school district. If you choose another book, remember to tell your students the reason that the book you chose was banned—not, "A group of pinheads who can barely read said we can't read this," but "The district has decided that we will remove this book, based on parental objections." If students want details, you can say, "I recommend that you talk to your parents." Stop there. You do not want to risk being quoted out of context and thereby inflaming emotions.

(Over the years various communities have banned all kinds of books, many of which have been recognized as classics—*The Adventures of Tom Sawyer, To Kill a Mockingbird, Flowers for Algernon, Anne Frank: The Diary of a Young Girl, Tales of a Fourth Grade Nothing*—the list, unfortunately, goes on and on. We typically don't think of librarians as being a subversive group, but several I know routinely schedule "Banned Book Week," during which these and other such books are placed on prominent display in the school library. "Celebrate the First Amendment," the sign says. "Read a banned book!" Kids love it.)

We have all known or read about teachers who have found themselves the target of various groups associated with the religious right. (Maybe there's also a "religious left," but I've never seen them picketing a school to have students read more books promoting tolerance, diversity, and inclusiveness, or carrying signs proclaiming "Darwin Was Right!" Maybe they need to get organized...) This is a conservative time in education, and the current focus is on assessment and accountability. For some religious and political groups, the focus is also on conforming to standards that they set for themselves and would like to set for everybody else.

Teachers need to be proactive in alerting parents and administrators to possible controversy.

The pendulum will eventually swing back, of course. I'm hopeful that it won't be long before we are able to take a more reasoned, moderate approach to education—an approach that will include a certain amount of academic flexibility and a recognition that not everything a child learns has be tested—nor can it be. In the meantime, teachers need to be proactive in alerting parents and administrators to possible controversy so that they do not end up having to defend their classroom choices and their jobs without the support of their school system.

Besides trying to influence the curriculum to conform to his personal beliefs, the Caped Crusader may also want to influence other classroom practices for his own benefit or for the benefit of his own child.

> **Crusader:** Ben has a hard time getting up in the morning.
> **Teacher:** He's missing essential reading instruction several times a week.
> **Crusader:** I don't see why you can't just wait to start reading instruction until Ben gets here.

Clearly, no teacher should have to readjust the instruction schedule for everyone because one child wants to sleep in. However, on occasion, the Crusader will actually have a valid concern, one that may require understanding and creativity on the part of the teacher:

Crusader: I understand that you're taking all the fifth
graders to the petting zoo.

Teacher: Yes, we've just finished our animal unit and we're
looking forward to seeing the animals we've read about.

Crusader: You know, my son Donnie is allergic to animal hair.

Teacher: He is?

Crusader: Yes. So he won't be able to go. I don't think
it's fair that he isn't able to participate in a class
activity. He's going to feel left out. I would think
that if one child can't go, none of them should.

This kind of issue requires a sensitive response. "Okay, then, we'll call it off" isn't an option if you have 25 other 8-year-olds wait ing to pet Bambi. Calling it off will not improve Donnie's popularity with his classmates, either. Instead, you might try this approach:

Teacher: Would you like to come along with us that day?
Maybe there are some things your son can do on the
trip. There are interesting displays inside the farmhouse
and there's a video, too. The decision would be yours.

It's not always easy for the teacher to balance the needs of the minority against the rights of the majority, but it's the right thing to do. The thoughtful teacher will strive to find a way that all kids can participate in some meaningful way, if at all possible.

Sometimes, however, despite our best efforts, a parent cannot be assuaged. Suppose the conversation goes more like this:

Teacher: Maybe you'd like to come along that day.

It's not always easy for the teacher to balance the needs of the minority against the rights of the majority, but it's the right thing to do.

Maybe there are some things your son could do and
you would know what those things are.

Crusader: Look, I can't take off work for something
like this. There's no way my child can go and I insist
you cancel the trip.

Teacher: I'm sorry. That's just not possible.

Crusader: Well, I'll just have to see the principal.

Teacher: You need to do what you think is right.

*When you
plan ahead,
parents will be
grateful that you
considered the
needs of their
child, rather
than angry
that their
child may
be excluded.*

If you're lucky, the principal will support your choice. If not, the
principal can explain the situation to the parents of the other students so that your choices can be seen as school policy and not as
your individual choice.

As a side note, however, I'd like to add that today's teacher
should be familiar with students' medical issues as they affect classroom activities, so as to avoid some of these conflicts. If you know
ahead of time that certain children have asthma or allergies or any
condition that could affect their participation in a school activity, you
can take their needs into account when planning. When you plan
ahead, parents will be grateful that you considered the needs of their
child, rather than angry that their child may be excluded.

Sometimes teachers, especially new ones, are reluctant to bring
problems with insistent parents to their principal because they are
afraid that it will make them look incompetent. This is a mistake,
unless the principal himself is incompetent. (If so, you've got even
bigger problems.) Part of a principal's job is to deal with irate parents,
so let her do it. Another part of the principal's job is running inter-
ference so that you can do your job. If the Crusader continues to be
a problem, refer him to the principal on a regular basis.

If you really can't go to the principal, a veteran colleague may be able to help. He or she has probably weathered similar situations and not only can advise you, but can also be physically present at conferences—as both a buffer and a witness in a possibly volatile situation.

Here are some points to remember when dealing with the Crusader:

- All parents have the right to review what their child is learning and to opt out of some activities. Don't take their objections personally.

- Avoid some confrontations by being proactive and alerting parents to classroom assignments that might be viewed as controversial. Parents appreciate knowing about things before they happen. While they may not agree with your choices, they won't think that you're trying to push something past them without their noticing. By the same token, if parents ignore the information and protest your choice afterwards, you can always point to the fact that they were alerted beforehand.

- Schools need to have a policy on censorship. If your school doesn't have one, see if you can promote developing one. It's for your own protection.

- If problems persist, refer the Crusader to your principal.

It's important to remember that the Crusader sometimes has a point, even if his solution is unacceptable. Keep an open mind, and you may be able to work out a reasonable compromise. If you can't, you need to decide what is important to you and what is best for kids. It's not your job to resolve every difference with a parent; it's your job to teach. Get your principal involved and let him or her work it out.

If you can win over the Caped Crusader, you can harness his energy to do good and vanquish evil. When he believes in a cause, he can be a tireless worker. If you're lucky, you can get him to channel his efforts toward raising money for new playground equipment...or maybe even garnering support for the school budget.

MS. "QUIT PICKING ON MY KID"

Whenever a conflict arises, whatever the circumstances, some parents will accuse the teacher of picking on their child. Even when the parent admits that her child's behavior was unacceptable, she will argue that everyone else's was, too. "Unless you're going to punish everyone," she will tell the teacher, "you shouldn't be singling out my child."

If you do punish the whole class, she will ask you to single her child out as the only one who doesn't deserve it. (Of course, punishing the whole class is a bad idea anyway, and I'd like to think that there are no teachers left on the planet who would ever do that.)

Here's an example of a conversation with Ms. "Quit Picking on My Kid!":

Ms. Quit: I understand you told Amanda that her T-shirt wasn't acceptable and she shouldn't wear it to school again.

Teacher: Yes, that's true.

Ms. Quit: Well, what about all the other kids who wear the same kind of shirts?

Teacher: What other kids?

Parent: I could stand in the hall and see ten kids with shirts worse than hers. Why are you just picking on my daughter?

Teacher: You can find ten kids whose t-shirts say something worse than "I put the F-U in Fun?"

Parent: It's part of a song.

Teacher: We don't let kids wear t-shirts like that.

Parent: I think she has a right to wear whatever she wants. If everyone else can, so can she.

Of course, the first question in the teacher's mind is usually, "Why would a parent defend her child's 'right' to be offensive?" The second question is, "What in the world are the lyrics to the *rest* of that song?"

I can't answer either one of those questions, but I do know that the teacher in the example above allowed herself to be distracted from the main issue. The school rules about dress are not personal, and they apply to all kids. Let's try it again:

Parent: I understand you told Amanda her T-shirt was not acceptable and she couldn't wear it to school again.

Teacher: Yes, that's true. Our school dress code says that students may not wear T-shirts with messages or pictures that are suggestive or offensive.

Parent: Well, what about the other kids?

Teacher: The issue here is Amanda's shirt. It violates the dress code about offensive messages.

Parent: Other kids do the same thing.

Teacher: The dress code prohibits shirts like these.

Parent: I think you're singling Amanda out.

Teacher: The dress code applies to everyone. No offensive T-shirts.

Parent: I could go outside and pick out ten kids with the same kind of shirt.

Teacher: Let me give you a copy of the dress code.

The "broken record" technique—repeating the same thing in different ways and staying on message—isn't new, but is still effective.

The "broken record" technique—repeating the same thing in different ways and staying on message—isn't new, but is still effective. It requires self-discipline. The teacher must refuse to be drawn into battle over whether or not the student has been singled out.

Here's another example:

Teacher: We can't tolerate Brian's use of the *F* word.

Parent: He's not the only one who swears.

Teacher: His language isn't appropriate for school.

Parent: Other kids swear.

Teacher: He will not be allowed to use language like that in my classroom.

Parent: What about all the other kids?

Teacher: I don't want any kids swearing in my classroom, and that includes Brian.

I have to admit that some parents have a point when they wonder whether a school rule is being applied equally to all students. What they don't understand is that it is tough, if not impossible, to catch every dress code violation or to discipline every student who uses foul language. Also, like it or not, some kids develop a track record that makes them more likely than others to be cited for yet another violation.

That being said, teachers need to be vigilant about applying the rules as equitably as possible. However, let's face it: even the most "objective" rules are open to interpretation. Here's another version of the conversation between Amanda's mother and the teacher:

Parent: I understand you told Amanda that she couldn't wear her T-shirt to school again.

Teacher: Yes, that's true. Our school dress code says that students may not wear T-shirts with messages or pictures that are suggestive or offensive.

Teachers need to be vigilant about applying the rules as equitably as possible.

It's not a bad idea for a teacher to admit that, despite her best efforts, the results are not always perfect.

Parent: Well, what about the other kids?

Teacher: The issue here is Amanda's shirt. It violates the dress code about offensive messages.

Parent: Other kids do the same thing. Nobody says anything to them.

Teacher: You know, it's not always possible to catch every violation every day. We do our best to make sure that kids dress appropriately, but I'm not going to tell you that we see everything. We have 800 students in this school, and it's hard to catch everything. But we try.

Parent: I just don't want you to be picking on only Amanda.

Teacher: I understand. But I'd appreciate it if Amanda didn't wear that shirt again.

Parent: Okay. But you need to look at the other kids, too.

It's not a bad idea for a teacher to admit that, despite her best efforts, the results are not always perfect. It's even likely that Amanda herself has slipped by unnoticed in the past—maybe with this same shirt. However, part of the teacher's job is enforcing the dress code, and she needs to do it.

Sometimes the issue isn't dress, but behavior. Some parents may believe that their children are being denied a "right" they think others have:

Parent: I'd like to know what the problem is with Ralph waiting for his friends after school.

Principal: If students don't have a reason to be here, they need to go home when classes are over. No loitering.

Parent: Ralph has a reason to be here. He's waiting for his friends.

Principal: That's not a reason.

Parent: What do you mean, "That's not a reason?"
Waiting for his friends isn't a reason?

Principal: Students staying after school need to be with
a teacher or a coach. They just can't hang around in
the halls.

Parent: Like he's the only one in the halls after school!
Come on!

It's important to remember that parents don't have the advantage of seeing how their child's behavior multiplied by 20 or 50 or 100 other kids plays out. One kid waiting for a friend after school truly is no big deal. Fifty kids is. Let's try it again:

Parent: Ralph has a reason to be here. He's waiting for
his friends.

Principal: We can't allow students to be in the school
unsupervised. It's for our protection and for theirs.

Parent: I don't see how waiting for his friends is a problem.

Principal: It wouldn't be a problem if it were just
Ralph. But we have a number of kids who want to
hang around after school unsupervised and that *is* a
problem. It's an opportunity for kids to get into trouble, and I don't want that to happen to Ralph.

Parent: Well, I'm not sure I agree, but I see what you're
saying.

Most parents rarely think about what would happen if everyone did what they want to do, or what their child wants to do. This is understandable; they are focusing on their own needs. As teachers, though, we know that

behavior can be contagious. If we let one second grader get a drink of
water during the spelling test, the next thing you know we have a
drought. If one kid throws up on the school bus, we're one block
away from a barf-o-rama.

We need to help parents understand that rules are made for
everyone's benefit, even though it may not look like it at first glance.
An example:

*We need to
help parents
understand that
rules are made
for everyone's
benefit, even
though it may
not look like
it at first glance.*

> **Mom:** I'll come down to the classroom to pick up Curt
> for his allergy shots.
>
> **Teacher:** Actually, our school policy is that you should
> go to the nurse's office, and she will call Curt down.
>
> **Mom:** I'd rather just come down to the room. It's
> quicker.
>
> **Teacher:** We try not to have parents come to the room.
> It's a disruption for the other students.
>
> **Mom:** I don't see how picking up my own child is such
> a big deal. Going to the nurse's office is an incon-
> venience.
>
> **Teacher:** I understand. But we have lots of students
> who have doctor's or dentist's appointments during
> the day. If all parents came directly to their child's
> room, we'd have a steady stream of interruptions.
> Also, for safety reasons in this day and age, we really
> don't want a lot of adults wandering the halls.
>
> **Mom:** Oh. I guess I hadn't thought about that.

If you take the time to explain to a parent why a particular rule
must be followed, most will accept the idea, even if they don't agree
with it. Unfortunately, this is not always the case:

> **Parent:** You had no right to take Alicia's cell phone away.

Teacher: She was talking on the phone during my math
class.

Parent: She was talking to me! She just called to tell me
she'd be late from school.

Teacher: I understand. But we were in the middle of
math class. We can't have kids interrupting class
with phone calls.

Parent: Other students have phones in class. You are
singling her out!

Teacher: Other students do have phones. But she was
the only one talking on one.

Parent: That phone is her personal property and I want
it back right now!

Teacher: Of course. Here it is. As I told her, she can
have it back after school. Please remind her not to
use it in class.

Parent: I'm not reminding her of anything.

If you take the time to explain to a parent why a particular rule must be followed, most will accept the idea, even if they don't agree with it.

Despite the parent's parting comment, it's unlikely that Alicia will use her phone again in math class unless she decides on a deliberate challenge to her teacher's authority. If that happens, the stakes are raised, and the problem needs to be moved to the principal's office.

Up to this point we've talked about dealing with parents who think their child is being singled out because of the child's behavior. Sometimes, however, if a student is not performing as well as the parents would like academically, the parents may accuse the teacher of singling the student out in other ways. Parents may complain that the teacher is expecting more (or less) from their child than from other students, that the teacher is being harder (or easier) on him than on other students. The bottom line is that parents may believe that their child is not getting the breaks that other students are. Here's an example:

Teacher: I just don't think Sam will be successful in AP
English next year. I think he should stay with regular
English.

Parent: We want him to take AP.

Teacher: Does he want to take AP?

Parent: It doesn't matter what he wants.

Teacher: AP takes a lot of work and effort. Sam doesn't
seem willing to work hard in English.

Parent: He'll work hard for teachers he likes. He feels
that you pick on him.

Teacher: I don't pick on him. I do get after him about
his homework.

Parent: He's not the only one who doesn't do it.

Parents need to be reassured that their child is not being singled out or excluded for no reason.

Parents need to be reassured that their child is not being singled
out or excluded for no reason. They need to feel secure that the
teacher's recommendations are in their child's best interests and not
simply the result of the teacher's need to be right.

Here's a more productive way to handle the previous conversation:

Parent: Sam works hard for teachers he likes. He feels
that you pick on him.

Teacher: I'm sorry he feels that way. I do get after him
about his homework.

Parent: He's not the only one who doesn't do it.

Teacher: I know. I wish I had only one student I had to
get after. But that's my job, and I'm sure you wouldn't
like it if I just ignored it.

Parent: Well, what about AP?

Teacher: If you really want him to take the course, he
can sign up. I'll meet with him individually and talk
to him about the course expectations.

Parent: I'll talk to him, too.

I strongly suggest that if a parent insists on his child taking a course over the teacher's objection, the teacher should let him sign up. Maybe the teacher's wrong—he should hope that he is. Maybe taking the AP course isn't the best thing for the student, but it won't be the worst thing that ever happened to him, either.

It isn't always easy to deflect a parent's charge that a teacher is picking on her child. After all, what the parent is really questioning is the teacher's fairness, even professionalism. Many teachers naturally become defensive. However, defensiveness that results in responding directly to a parent's challenge is the worst response.

Parent: Penny says you pick on her when she's not paying attention.

Teacher: I don't pick on her.

Parent: Well, she feels picked on. She thinks you don't like her.

Teacher: I do like her.

Parent: She thinks you let other kids get away with things, but not her.

Teacher: I don't let other kids get away with things.

Parent: Well, that's how she feels—that you pick on her.

Teacher: I don't pick on her.

"Yes, you are! No, I'm not"— sounds like two kids on the playground. Clearly, simple denial doesn't work. Here's a different approach:

Parent: Penny says you pick on her in class.

Teacher: What does that mean?

Parent: I don't know. She just says you pick on her.

Teacher: Hmmm. I wonder how she defines being
picked on.

Parent: I don't really know the specifics. She doesn't say.

Teacher: Well, that would be important. I'd like to
know what she means.

Parent: I guess you'll have to ask her.

Teacher: Maybe you could ask her. Or maybe we could
meet with her together. This is something I take seriously, because I work hard to treat kids fairly.

Parent: Well, maybe I'll talk to her and then let you know.

*A good technique
for a teacher
to employ is to
ask the parent
to define her
terms.*

Rather than accepting the charge on the face of it, a good technique for a teacher to employ is to ask the parent to define her terms.
What does "picking on" mean to your child? That you won't let her
talk while you're talking? That you won't accept late homework? That
you expect her to keep her hands and feet to herself? Rather than
quickly trying to defend your actions, it's a good idea to stop, think,
and then ask questions first to clarify what exactly the parent means.
Don't deny. Clarify:

Parent: John says you give way too much homework. He
just can't get it all done.

Teacher: I don't give too much homework.

No, no, no! Remember: Don't deny. Clarify.

Parent: John says you give way too much homework.
He just can't get it all done.

Teacher: How much homework does he think he could do?

Parent: Ahhhhhhh ... geez, I don't know. An hour?

Teacher: Well, I typically give about a half hour.

Parent: Well, he says it takes him an hour.

Teacher: Do you check his assignments in the evening?

Parent: Not usually. Should I?

Teacher: It might not be a bad idea. Maybe you could
monitor his homework for a week or so and then we
can meet again.

If you can remember that both you and the parent want the same
thing—the child's success in school—you may be able to stay out of the
win-lose arena. It's not easy, but it can be done by refusing to be
defensive. Don't respond directly to a parent's accusations.

It's also helpful to keep in the back of your mind that the parent
just might have a point. You may think it's an itty bitty point, but it's
a point nonetheless. Ignoring that possibility can leave you blindsided
and may exacerbate what begins as a small problem. So let's consider
this possibility for a moment:

What if the parent is right?

So far in this chapter we've talked about how to respond professionally when parents accuse a teacher of picking on their child or
singling him out for one reason or another. We've talked about how
parents can have myopic vision when it comes to their own child,
finding it difficult to imagine how their child's behavior multiplied
by 50 kids can present a problem in the school. We also talked about
how school rules are generally made for the greater good, so that all
children can learn without disruption or interruption. We believe
that school rules should be based on the golden mean: what would
the result be if everyone took this action?

Having said all of the above, I should point out that teachers still
need to be careful about using that old chestnut, "If I let your child
(fill in the blank), I'd have to let everyone's child (fill in the blank
with the same words)." For example, "If I let your child bring a pony

*It's also helpful to
keep in the back
of your mind
that the parent
just might
have a point.*

to school, I'd have to let everyone's child bring a pony." In this case, the parent can understand how (assuming that every child had a pony) it could be distracting with the noise and the manure and all. But in some cases, the parent may think, "Yeah, so what?" We need to be careful that the rules are really made for the good of the students, *not* for the convenience of the teacher.

The charge of singling kids out (or the converse, not responding to a child's individual needs) is among the most common complaints parents have. Before dismissing such a complaint out of hand, it's a good idea to listen carefully and reflectively to be sure that your response isn't based on convenience or a need for control. Here's a worst case example of what happens when a rule or procedure is not based on what's best for kids:

We need to be careful that the rules are really made for the good of the students, not for the convenience of the teacher.

Parent: I'd like my daughter to be able to take whatever book she wants out of the library.

Librarian: I choose the books for second graders. She can pick from the second grade shelf.

Parent: She can read at a 10th grade level!

Librarian: If I let your daughter choose any book in the library, I'd have to let all the second graders choose any book.

Parent: And the problem with that is...?

Librarian: Not all second graders can read as well as your daughter. They would take out books they couldn't understand. And I'll be the one reshelving them.

Parent: What if I told you I don't care?

Librarian: Your daughter still has to pick from the second grade books.

Behind each rule should be a genuine reason that isn't really based on our own comfort level, but on the good of our classes as a whole. Basing decisions on what's best for the teacher instead of what's best for the students is simply wrong.

Here's another example of how a teacher's need to be in control can get in the way:

Parent: Zach occasionally has back spasms. He may need to get up and walk around.

Teacher: That could be a problem.

Parent: When he can move, he can listen. You may not think he's paying attention, but he is. He just needs to move.

Teacher: If I let Zach get up and move, I'll have to let all the students do it.

Of course, that's not true. Kids know instinctively when another student has a special need of some kind. Most of them have an innate sense of fairness. If a child has a special need that we can easily accommodate, we should do it. Here's a more reasonable approach:

Parent: Zach occasionally has back spasms. He may need to get up and walk around.

Teacher: All he has to do is give me a little signal. We can make this work.

If we are unwilling to respond to a child's genuine need to be singled out for extra attention or assistance, even supportive parents can be trained to become difficult.

Let's review the techniques with parents who accuse you of picking on their child or singling him or her out in a negative sense:

*Insist that
parents define
their terms.
What does
"picking on"
look like?
How long is
an assignment
that is "too
long"?*

- Be a broken record. If it's a rule that you must enforce, stay on message. If it's behavior that simply cannot be tolerated—bullying, loitering, foul language, disrespect—teachers and administrators need to stay the course, but work to convince parents that the rules are applied the same to all.

- Help parents see that their child's behavior, multiplied by many students, can be a problem. One child arriving early can stand quietly in the doorway. Fifty kids need supervision.

- Insist that parents define their terms. What does "picking on" look like? How long is an assignment that is "too long"?

- Make sure the rules are for the good of children and the school in general, not just for the teacher's convenience or need to control.

- Make adjustments for individual kids who need it and don't worry about upsetting the classroom.

Parents sometimes act as if teachers and administrators like telling kids what they can or can't wear. Or that we like hounding kids to turn in their homework.

They're dead wrong, of course. Why would anyone spend all those years in college just to spend a lifetime doing that?

THE INTIMIDATOR

Many people think that teachers can be intimidators—and they can be. The teacher who holds a student up to ridicule, bullies a student in gym class, yells at a first grader, or embarrasses or even threatens a student—none of these people belong in the classroom.

Parents can be intimidators in the classroom, too, although they are usually more subtle:

Teacher: Thanks for meeting with me, Mr. Kozinski.

Intimidator: Well, I hope you can make this quick, Alice.

Teacher: I'll do the best I can, but I really need to talk to you about Ronnie's behavior in class.

Intimidator: *(Silence)*

Teacher: *(nervously)* He's very disrespectful.

Intimidator: *(Silence.)*

Teacher: He makes it difficult for the others to learn.

Intimidator: I really find that hard to believe.

Teacher: Yesterday, for example, he kept making monkey noises every time I turned my back.

Intimidator: You know, Alice, I have a lot more important things to do than hear about how my son makes
monkey noises. It seems to me a good teacher wouldn't
have that problem.

It is important to establish in a parent conversation that teacher
and parent are equals. In the above conversation, the teacher calls the
parent "Mr." while the parent calls the teacher "Alice." Instead of
being a conversation between equals, it is more like a conversation
between a restaurant diner and his server for the evening.

See how this changes the tone:

*It is
important
to establish
in a parent
conversation
that teacher
and parent
are equals.*

Teacher: Thanks for meeting with me, Mr. Kozinski.

Intimidator: Well, I hope you can make this quick, Alice.

Teacher: I know you're a busy person, Bob, so let me
get right to it. Your son's grades are suffering because
he is having trouble staying on task.

Intimidator: What does that mean?

Teacher: It means that instead of listening to directions, he's busy trying to entertain the other kids.
I've talked to him several times and I've moved him
to the front of the room. I've even kept him after
school. I think he needs to hear from you that he
needs to settle down.

Intimidator: I'll tell him that.

Notice what the teacher does in this conversation:

- She immediately switches to a first name basis. If the
  parent calls her Alice, she must be able to call him
  Bob.

- She acknowledges that "Bob" is busy, and cuts to the
  chase.

- She focuses on the result of the child's behavior—low
  grades.

- She tells what actions she's already taken.

- She tells the parent specifically what she wants him
  to do.

Calling a parent by his or her first name may take a little courage, but with practice a teacher can do it. Before you meet with a parent or call him on the phone, it's a good idea to be sure you know his first name, just in case he decides to call you by yours. (A side note: it's never safe to assume that a parent's surname is the same as the child's, so always check.)

It's important that the teacher point out what she's done so far to correct the student's behavior. Talking to the parent shouldn't be the first step in dealing with an unruly child:

Talking to the parent shouldn't be the first step in dealing with an unruly child.

Intimidator: How can you allow him to make monkey
    noises?

Teacher: I've spoken to him and I've moved his seat to
    the front of the room. He's also lost play time at the
    end of the day because of his behavior. I hate to
    send him home, but we're heading that way unless
    his behavior improves.

Intimidator: Ronnie and I will have a conversation and
    you will see an improvement.

Intimidators may be used to getting what they want and are clear in their expectations for you. However, they may not be so clear when it comes to expectations for their child. Notice how the Intimidator in the following conversation puts all responsibility on the teacher and none on the child:

Intimidator: What does Beth have to do to raise her
grade in this class?

Teacher: She'll need to get her homework in on time
and study for the tests.

Intimidator: I would expect you to see that she does
that.

Teacher: I will do my best, but some of it is up to her.

Intimidator: You're the teacher. It's your job to see that
she works hard.

Make sure you start out with and maintain a professional tone.

Intimidators are often people who are used to being in charge
and telling subordinates what to do. Sometimes they view teachers
not as professionals, but as public servants—with the emphasis on the
servant part. Make sure you start out with and maintain a professional tone. It helps to remember that the Intimidator wouldn't
dream of talking to his doctor the way he talks to his child's teacher.
Imagine a conversation like this:

Intimidator: So I'll expect to see an improvement in
my daughter's flu.

Doctor: Only if she takes her medicine and follows my
instructions regarding rest.

Intimidator: I'm going out of town. I expect you to see
that she does those things.

Doctor: Next patient!

Keep in mind that "medical model" when you meet with the
Intimidator. Don't let the Intimidator get away with expecting you to
do his job. It's useful to clearly point out the role that he has in helping his child be successful in school.

Intimidator: So I'll expect to see an improvement in
Liz's grades.

Teacher: I will do my best to help her, but whether she improves depends on her. And you.

Intimidator: Me? You're the teacher!

Teacher: If you make it clear to Liz that you expect her best effort, that will certainly help.

Intimidator: Well, I'm out of town a lot. I can talk to her, but it's still up to you to see that her work is done.

Teacher: I'll do my best. But no one is more effective with a child than her mother or father.

Intimidator: She knows what my expectations are.

Teacher: Good. It probably wouldn't hurt to tell her, though, that we've talked and that you're aware of what she needs to do.

Intimidator: All right. But I'll be looking for some improvement in her grade the next time.

Teacher: I hope you tell her that.

Intimidator: You need to tell her that, too.

Intimidators will sometimes threaten teachers, saying that they will go to the principal or the superintendent or the school board if they don't get what they want. There's only one good response to such a threat:

Teacher: You need to do what you think is right.

Never try to talk a parent out of going over your head. Intimidators can smell fear. "Do what you think is right" means, "I am sticking to my guns. If the principal wants me to do something different, I'll be answering to him and not to you." Then be sure to alert your supervisor that he or she may be getting a call.

Even when Intimidators raise the threat level with, "You'll hear from my lawyer," the response should be the same:

Teacher: You need to do what you think is right.

Sometimes the Intimidator will even make the Ultimate Threat:

Intimidator: Well, it looks like we'll just have to pull Evan out and send him to private school.
Teacher: Yippee! Woo hoo! Happy dance!

Of course, that's only going on in the teacher's head. In reality, here's what she should say:

Teacher: I'm sorry to hear that. I hope he'll like it.

Here are a few other ways for teachers to avoid or diffuse intimidating situations:

If a child commits a flagrant foul that results in discipline, call the parent before the student gets home.

- The best defense is a good offense. If a child commits a flagrant foul that results in discipline, call the parent before the student gets home. If you wait, you may receive an angry call before you have a chance to tell the parent what really happened. Parents deserve the courtesy of a phone call, and it's better to put the errant student in the position of having to explain himself.

- Never force a child to call his parent to tell what he's done wrong while you stand right over him. This move is popular with some elementary and middle school teachers, but it can backfire. In the first place, it smacks of bullying on the part of the teacher. In the second place, the parent may balk at the implied expectation that she should respond in some predetermined way to what she is hearing from her child. Is she supposed to be angry? Apologetic? Disappointed? If she simply accepts the information to deal with when the child gets home, does she look like she doesn't care? If you want to keep the lines of communication open and work with the parent to solve a problem, it is much better to deal with classroom issues adult to adult.

- Try not to take an irate phone call at the end of the day. Parents sometimes overreact by calling the school as soon as the child gets off the bus and tells his story. If they believe their child has been wronged in some way, they may be too angry to engage in reasoned dialogue. Wait until the following morning when everyone has had time to cool off. Then you make the call. Don't wait for the parents to call a second time.

Parents sometimes overreact by calling the school as soon as the child gets off the bus and tells his story.

- Do not give parents your home phone number or, God forbid, your cell phone number. Even if it seems like a good idea at the time, it is not. You need to separate your personal and professional lives. Besides, e-mail works just as well—maybe better—because you can open it or not, as you choose. (If you choose to respond by e-mail, NO SHOUTING!)

Bullies are the same whether they're six or thirty-six. It's sometimes hard to keep your wits about you when a bully challenges you. But remember: you have stood up to intimidating behavior before—perhaps your older brother, a college roommate, the head of your department.

You're a teacher. You're brave by definition.

THE STEALTH ZAPPER

Unlike the Intimidator, who lets you know exactly where he stands and what he wants, the Stealth Zapper gently implies that you (or maybe a colleague) aren't quite up to snuff. Her comments and criticisms fly so low under the radar that you may not realize you have been zapped until you stop to consider what she has said. She may appear innocent, but her words and actions can sting.

The Stealth Zapper can appear to be a big supporter of the school, but only if it enhances her child's opportunities. She works hard to ingratiate herself with teachers if she thinks it might give her child an advantage. For example, if her child tries out for the musical, she will volunteer to be the accompanist for auditions. If her child gets a big part, look for this parent behind the scenes building sets, making costumes, and selling tickets at the door. If her child gets a smaller part, she will still be there, but she will probably be pointing out the director's mistakes at every opportunity. Conversations are likely to go something like this:

Stealth Zapper: It's too bad that Marion is so much taller than Harold Hill. It's kind of hard to believe they're a couple.

Teacher: *(thinking)* This is an eighth grade production of *The Music Man*. All the girls are taller than the boys! *(aloud)* Marion has the strongest voice in the class.

Stealth Zapper: I don't think you gave Brooklyn a chance to show you what she can really do.

Teacher: We listened to all the students sing at auditions.

Stealth Zapper: Yes, but I think you were talking to someone during her audition.

Generally, the best approach with the Stealth Zapper is to deal with her directly, hold your ground, and be polite.

Unlike the Intimidator, who puts an issue right on the table (or right in the teacher's face), the Stealth Zapper obliquely criticizes what the teacher has done and is more subtle in asking for what she wants. Here's another example of how she can catch a teacher off guard:

Stealth Zapper: Marjorie was so disappointed when you gave her a C– on her project.

Teacher: *(thinking)* What's the right answer to that? That's what she deserved? I'm sorry to disappoint her? She should have worked harder and gotten it in on time? And I didn't "give" her anything! *(aloud)* I'm sorry to hear that.

Stealth Zapper: She really didn't understand the directions. They weren't very clear.

Teacher: *(thinking)* We only went over them a million times! *(aloud)* I'm sorry to hear that.

Generally, the best approach with the Stealth Zapper is to deal with her directly, hold your ground, and be polite. Here's a better approach:

Stealth Zapper: Marjorie was really disappointed when you gave her a C– on her project.

Teacher: Really.

Stealth Zapper: She didn't understand the directions. They weren't very clear.

Teacher: I'm surprised to hear that. She never asked for clarification.

Stealth Zapper: You know how shy Marjorie is.

Teacher: Yes. But it's hard to know that a student doesn't understand something if she doesn't speak up.

Another ploy the Stealth Zapper uses to try to ingratiate herself with her child's current teacher is to subtly (or not so subtly) denigrate the last teacher her child had:

Stealth Zapper: Marjorie loves your class. Last year she had a really hard time in English.

Teacher: Really? Why is that?

Stealth Zapper: Mr. Johnson was so strict. He just had no sense of humor. Not like you, according to Marjorie.

The teacher may be trying to imagine either Marjorie or her mother appreciating a good sense of humor—or he may be wondering if either one would be amused to know that Mr. Johnson was his college roommate and best man at his wedding!

Comments about colleagues should also be dealt with directly, if possible. Here's an example:

Stealth Zapper: Miss Truman was so strict. None of the kids liked her. She just had no sense of humor. Marjorie thinks you're really funny.

Teacher: Well, I'm surprised. Miss Truman is known for her sense of humor. Kids usually love it.

Comments about colleagues should also be dealt with directly, if possible.

But what if the last time Miss Truman laughed out loud was 1978, and her sense of humor is so dry that it's parched? You still need to avoid any appearance of agreeing with her criticism. If you aren't comfortable defending Miss Truman or another teacher, remember that an equally effective strategy is to just ignore the Stealth Zapper's personal observations and respond only to those that pertain to you.

*No matter
what you think
of a colleague,
you need to
remain positive
or at least
noncommittal
when the
Stealth Zapper
criticizes
another
teacher.*

Stealth Zapper: Miss Truman was so strict. She had no
    sense of humor. Not like you, according to Marjorie.

Teacher: I'm glad Marjorie gets my jokes. I enjoy having
    her in class.

No matter what you think of a colleague, you need to remain positive or at least noncommittal when the Stealth Zapper criticizes another teacher. Not only is it unprofessional to denigrate a colleague, but it also gives the Stealth Zapper ammunition to use at another time with another teacher. None of these teacher responses needs to be delivered in anything other than a conversational tone of voice. You just want to be sure the Stealth Zapper understands that you don't accept her implications about your colleagues.

Stealth Zapper: I'm so glad Jimmy got you for a teacher
    instead of Mr. Golden. They say he's never prepared
    for class.

Teacher: *(thinking about seeing Mr. Golden doing a cross-
    word puzzle during his prep period)* Well, I hope Jimmy
    enjoys biology this year.

Notice that you are not defending Mr. Golden nor acknowledging the accuracy of the Zapper's statement. You are just focusing on your own interaction with this child. If you stick with this strategy, the parent will eventually get the message that you are not a person who engages in small talk with parents about colleagues.

Here's another example:

Stealth Zapper: What do you think of your new principal? He doesn't seem to like kids.

Teacher: *(refusing to take the bait)* Actually, he's a great guy. The kids really like him.

Even if the parent has verbalized exactly what you think, too, remember that you are not required to respond to questions that are essentially inappropriate.

Stealth Zapper: What do you think of your new principal? He doesn't seem to like kids.

Here are some possible responses:

Teacher: I really haven't heard that.

or

Teacher: I'd think you'd have to like kids to be a principal.

or

Teacher: Being a principal is a tough job. You can't please everyone.

or

Teacher: He's still new to the school and not everyone knows him yet.

or

Teacher: If you think it's such an easy job, you ought to try it!

Okay, maybe not that last one.

What if the Stealth Zapper persists and asks you outright what you think of a colleague? Respond firmly:

Stealth Zapper: Don't you think the administration should do something about Ms. Roberts? I can't believe the stories I hear about her outside of school!

Teacher: Honestly, I just never make comments about other teachers.

Then stick with that response.

The Stealth Zapper may surreptitiously complain to a supervisor about you or another teacher. This is when she becomes more dangerous than annoying. Here's an example of a typical phone call:

Stealth Zapper: This is Ms. Zapper. My son Kevin is in Mr. Jackson's biology class.

Principal: What can I do for you, Ms. Zapper?

Stealth Zapper: I hate to complain, but Mr. Jackson's last test was completely unfair.

Principal: In what way?

Stealth Zapper: Mr. Jackson had things on that test that he'd never even covered. Just about everyone in the class failed it.

Principal: I'll look into it.

Stealth Zapper: There is one other thing. I don't want you to use my name. I'm afraid if Mr. Jackson knows I've complained, he'll take it out on Kevin.

With some principals, this move is very effective. These are the principals who were absent when they handed out personal courage. They will actually bring up this issue with the teacher and refuse to

The Stealth Zapper may surreptitiously complain to a supervisor about you or another teacher. This is when she becomes more dangerous than annoying.

divulge the name of the complainer. This administrative behavior is not only patently unfair to the teacher but is also guaranteed to make the principal the hot topic in the faculty room the next day. By agreeing to the Stealth Zapper's terms, he implicitly concurs that Mr. Jackson *would* take it out on poor Kevin.

An effective principal would handle the Stealth Zapper more like this:

Stealth Zapper: There is one other thing. I don't want you to use my name. I'm afraid if Mr. Jackson knows I've complained, he'll take it out on Kevin.

Principal: I'm sorry. If you're unwilling to let me use your name, there's nothing I can do about this.

Stealth Zapper: I can't believe that you refuse to investigate this issue!

Principal: I'm sure Mr. Jackson would want to know if Kevin had a problem with his test. Perhaps the best thing would be for you to set up an appointment with Mr. Jackson yourself to discuss it.

Stealth Zapper: I'll have to think about it.

Teachers have a right to know if a parent has a concern, and which parent it is—not so they can take it out on the student, but so that they can judge whether or not the source is credible. It is easy for a parent to impugn a teacher to the principal, who will probably not know the students as well as the teacher and thus be less able to judge the validity of the complaint.

Principals and other supervisors need to insist that complaints from parents about grades or homework go directly to the teacher first. It's the professional way of handling a concern and shows respect for the teacher. If your principal doesn't insist on this rule for

*Principals
and other
supervisors
need to insist
that complaints
from parents
about grades
or homework
go directly to
the teacher
first.*

ordinary complaints, you can sometimes politely and respectfully suggest that course of action:

> Principal: One of your parents complained about your
> test.
> Teacher: Really? Who?
> Principal: I can't really say.
> Teacher: Because you don't know?
> Principal: No, I know who it is. I just promised her I
> wouldn't tell you who it is.
> Teacher: Because then she'd have to kill you?

Okay, say that only if you know for sure that the principal has a
sense of humor and you won't get fired. If there's even the slightest
doubt about either of those issues, try something like this instead:

> Teacher: It's hard to respond to that kind of criticism
> when you don't know who the student is.
> Principal: Well, they said the test was on material you
> didn't cover.
> Teacher: Which questions? What material? Which test?
> Principal: I really don't know.
> Teacher: You know, maybe the parent should just call
> and talk to me. It's impossible to respond or give you
> any information if I don't know the specifics.
> Principal: She doesn't want to talk to you.
> Teacher: Because...?
> Principal: Uh...She thinks you'll take it out on her child.
> Teacher: You're kidding.
> Principal: Look, I'll tell her she has to call you.

It may not go exactly like that, but eventually the principal will
realize he's on shaky ground. If not, try this:

*If you are
the target of
an anonymous
complaint, refuse
to accept the
premise of the
complaint until
you explore
where it came
from.*

Principal: She doesn't want to talk to you.

Teacher: Well, that's too bad because it's easy to lodge an anonymous complaint. I really can't respond to something like that.

Principal: Did you give a test recently?

Teacher: Yes, I did. But the grades ranged from 54 to 100, so I really don't know what the issue is.

Principal: I'll get back to you.

Though you still may not find out who made the complaint, at least you will have made your position clear—that you cannot respond to anonymous complaints.

When dealing with the Stealth Zapper, remember these tips:

*   Be careful of appearing to accept her insinuations, especially about colleagues. If you consistently refute or refuse to respond to her innuendoes, she will eventually stop using them.

*   If you are the target of an anonymous complaint, refuse to accept the premise of the complaint until you explore where it came from. Explain to the principal or supervisor that it is impossible to know what exactly the parent means unless you know who the student is.

*   Don't spend any more time with the Stealth Zapper than is absolutely necessary. It's too hard to keep your guard up for an extended period of time.

The Stealth Zapper's real agenda is sometimes obvious, sometimes not. Whether she uses flattery or criticism, her goal is to achieve some kind of advantage for her child.

One Stealth Zapper I knew was effusive in her praise of the band director, making a point of telling the principal how lucky the school was to have him on staff. When the principal passed the compliment along, the band director laughed. "Last year when her son didn't make first chair, she didn't have a single good thing to say about me," he said. "This year, when her daughter wants to be drum major, I'm wonderful. I'm the same guy I was last year. Go figure."

THE UNCIVIL LIBERTARIAN

We know that students do not shed their rights at the schoolhouse door. Nor should they. But do these rights include passionate embraces, obscene messages on shirts, the F word in its many forms, hazing, bullying, fighting, and visible underwear? Most teachers and administrators think not. The Uncivil Libertarian, however, fights for what he insists is his child's inalienable right to any or all of these.

I'm pretty sure that wearing pants around the knees is not a right our forefathers and foremothers died to protect, but you wouldn't know it to listen to some parents:

Parent: Wearing low pants is the style.

Teacher: We don't need to see Andrew's boxers.

Parent: It's just the style.

Teacher: He can dress however he wants off campus.

Parent: He's just expressing his individuality! It's his right!

What is interesting to me is that when I see the same student working at the mall at his part-time job, he is wearing the uniform of the Fast Food Army, pants pulled up around his waist and maybe even belted. Kids don't seem to mind repressing their individuality for a few hours while they ask if you want fries with that. And they aren't taking your order with their hands in the back pocket of their girlfriend's jeans, either.

Defending a student's fashion choices is one thing, but some parents will even defend behaviors that suggest more serious problems later on:

*While children,
especially
adolescents,
are constantly
testing their
limits, they
want to know
what the rules
are and who's
in charge.*

Parent: It's not my son's fault if the little boy gave him
his lunch money.

Teacher: Your son bullied the boy into handing it over.

Parent: They're friends.

Teacher: Your son is in sixth grade and the other boy is
a second grader.

Parent: Are you saying my son is a bully?

Teacher: Not at all. He's an extortionist. An incipient
thug. A Soprano in training.

All right, all right—don't say that. You may *think* it, though, and hope that it doesn't appear in a little bubble above your head. Instead, try something like this:

Parent: Are you saying my son is a bully?

Teacher: I'm saying that a sixth grader shouldn't be taking a second grader's lunch money.

Here's another example of the Uncivil Libertarian defending his child's "right" to underage drinking:

Parent: So Emily was drinking on the senior trip. Big
deal. That's what the trip is for.

Advisor: That is not what the trip is for.

Parent: Oh, come on. You know they all drink.

Advisor: Kids and parents signed an agreement before
the kids left. The agreement specifically stated that
drinking was prohibited.

> Parent: That's not a legal document. You really can't
> hold anyone to that.

The Uncivil Libertarian may think that he is protecting his child when he defends bad behavior, but, in fact, he places his child in an untenable position between the two major authorities in his young life—his parent and his teacher. In addition, he sends a message that somehow the child's bad behavior will be tolerated by the rest of the world when he grows up.

While children, especially adolescents, are constantly testing their limits, they want to know what the rules are and who's in charge. They may not like the rules, but they still want them. In my experience, when a parent is rude to his child's teacher or principal in the child's presence, it doesn't make the child feel good—even if the child was rude just an hour or so before and that's the reason for the parent-teacher conversation in the first place.

The Uncivil Libertarian is often more difficult to deal with than his children, who by and large are fairly clear about the rules and how the system works. Students may not like the outcomes of their actions, but they are rarely surprised by them. While it is gratifying to a student that her parent will defend her, she really doesn't want her parent to look foolish in front of the teacher. It's sometimes beneficial to have the student sit in the conference with the parent. In the following conversation, the student's presence helps clarify the situation:

> Parent: So you're saying my daughter cheated on this
> assignment.
> Teacher: Instead of doing her own work, she cut and
> pasted paragraphs from a reference book.
> Parent: She probably didn't know she wasn't supposed
> to do that.

The Uncivil Libertarian is often more difficult to deal with than his children, who by and large are fairly clear about the rules and how the system works.

Teacher (to student): Keisha, did you know you weren't supposed to do that?

Keisha: Not really.

Teacher: Were you in class when we went to the computer lab and talked about this very thing?

Keisha: Yeah, but I didn't understand it.

Teacher: You didn't understand that you needed to do your own work?

Keisha: Other kids did the same thing.

Teacher: We're talking about you here. I don't accept this work from any student.

Parent: She wouldn't have done it if she had known.

Teacher: Keisha knows that if she had done the same thing by hand—copying other people's words directly out of a book and handing it in as her own—it would be wrong. Am I right, Keisha?

Keisha: Well, yeah, but this is different.

Teacher: The only difference is that you did it on the computer.

Parent: This technology is all so new. Kids may have a hard time seeing the difference.

Teacher: It is different from when you or I went to school. The technology isn't really new to kids, though. They have grown up with it.

Parent: I'm beginning to see what you mean, though. Do you, Keisha?

Keisha: Yeah.

Remember "deliver the message"? No confessions are necessary.

This is where the teacher should stop—just make the point and get out. Remember "deliver the message"? No confessions are necessary. You don't need to symbolically tie the student to a chair under a single light bulb and grill her. Keisha and her parent know what she has done, and they know it wasn't acceptable. It's time to move on to the problem solving phase:

Teacher: I'm willing to let Keisha do the assignment over.

Parent: Okay, fine. When exactly will it be due?

The major problem with the Uncivil Libertarian is his imperfect understanding of what constitutes a student's "right." He often confuses "right" with "want." He is one of the most difficult parents to deal with because reason rarely works. He is convinced that you are trying to take away some perceived "right," and his response to that injustice is often anger, as in the following example.

Parent: I want Buddy to be able to go on the Outdoors Club overnight trip to the nature center.

Teacher: The school rules are clear. Buddy was suspended for fighting, so he can't go.

Parent: He's been looking forward to this for weeks! He has a right to go.

Teacher: Participation in the overnight is not a right.

Parent: Well, I'd like to know how you can take something like this away from him when he really wants to go.

Teacher: I'm not taking it away. He's the one who got himself suspended.

Parent: It was the other kid's fault.

Teacher: I don't have anything to do with that. I just know Buddy can't go.

Parent: You haven't heard the last of this!

The teacher is left shaking her head. She may not be happy either. The timing is awful,

and she knows Buddy would have enjoyed the trip. However, the rules about participation in extracurricular activities are clear. She didn't make the rules, but she is required to follow them.

Since we are on the topic of angry parents, this is a good time to talk about setting limits in dealing with aggressive parents. Under no circumstances should a teacher respond in kind to a parent who has gone over the line. No yelling, swearing, or—god forbid—threatening to hit someone. However, when you have exhausted all of your professional resources, it's time to say, "Hasta la vista."

Under no circumstances should a teacher respond in kind to a parent who has gone over the line.

Suppose the meeting with Buddy's dad had gone like this:

Parent: Buddy is going on the overnight and you can't stop him.

Teacher: Actually, I know that if Buddy is suspended, he can't go.

Parent: You could take him if you wanted.

Teacher: Actually, I can't.

Parent: *(shouting)* I am sick and tired of listening to this garbage! If you were any kind of a teacher, you'd take him!

Teacher: You'll need to take this up with the administration. I'm finished here.

When a parent becomes at all abusive or out-of-control, it's time to end the conversation. Here's another example:

Parent: Who do you think you are, failing my Kelly?

Teacher: I didn't fail her. She refused to do the work.

Parent: Kelly may lose her scholarship because of you.

Teacher: It's not because of me. It's because of her.

Parent: You're the teacher. It's your fault.

Teacher: You were kept well aware of the situation.

Parent: If you weren't such a jerk, you would have
  passed her!
Teacher: *(rising)* This conversation is over.

You need to be polite, calm, and tolerant...up to a point. No one
expects you to take personal abuse. When any parent begins a personal attack, it's time to end the conference. Future conferences, if
any, should be held in the principal's office with the principal in
attendance.

Here are the points to remember when dealing with an Uncivil
Libertarian:

- Parents sometimes need to be educated regarding
  why a student's behavior is not acceptable. They still
  may not accept your reasons for your decisions, but
  you may assuage their anger when they understand
  the situation a little better.

- Try to be conciliatory, but still insist that the rules or
  school standards apply, whether or not the parent
  agrees with them.

- When parents become abusive or insulting, stop the
  conversation immediately. You may want to suggest
  that they take their concerns to the administration.

The Uncivil Libertarian unwittingly suggests a sense of entitle-
ment to his child. It is a disservice to the child. The world outside of
school simply won't buy it.

*When any
parent begins a
personal attack,
it's time to end
the conference.*

NO SHOW'S DAD

One truism about school is that you must be present to win. While being in school every day doesn't guarantee that a student will graduate with honors, not being there certainly decreases the chance that he will graduate at all. One kind of parent seems to think that attendance isn't mandatory, but optional. Here is a typical conversation with No Show's Dad:

No Show's Dad: We're taking Pete out of school for two weeks in
    March for a family vacation.
Teacher: You're taking him out while school is in session?
No Show's Dad: It's a lot cheaper to fly in March.
Teacher: He's going to miss two weeks of school!
No Show's Dad: That's why I'm telling you early. I'd like you to get all his
    work ready for him in advance so he can take it with him on vacation.

This request is difficult for a teacher. She really doesn't have time to prepare materials in advance for individual children, and she doesn't want to give the impression that two weeks of class time can be made up by completing a few assignments. She also knows that, if she does take the time to prepare all the materials for the absent child, it's unlikely that he will spend his time at Disney World completing his homework.

Still, she doesn't want to look as if she's unwilling to assist or
being punitive toward a child who really has no vote in the parent's
decision. In cases like this, it's usually best, despite her annoyance, to
provide what she can that is readily available.

> **No Show's Dad:** That's why I'm telling you early. I'd
> like you to get all his work ready for him in advance
> so he can take it with him on vacation.
>
> **Teacher:** *(thinking)* Fat chance. *(aloud)* I really don't
> think I'll have time to prepare special materials for
> your child ahead of time. I have some study guides
> prepared in advance, and he can take those with him
> along with the class novel. He'll miss all the math
> instruction, but maybe you can help him with some
> of the problems we'll be working on in class.

*It is difficult
for the teacher to
prevent absences
when they occur
with the full
consent (or even
encouragement)
of the parent.*

Taking students out of class for an extended period of time is rela-
tively rare. More often a student will be absent in smaller increments.
Here's an example of another kind of conversation with No Show's
Dad:

> **No Show's Dad:** I know there's a rule about having to
> be on time for school if you want to play in the game
> that night, but it was my fault Sam overslept.
>
> **Coach:** Sorry. He can't play.
>
> **No Show's Dad:** But it wasn't his fault!
>
> **Coach:** Sam is 17. He knows that he needs to get up.
>
> **No Show's Dad:** I don't see why my son is being
> penalized for something that was my fault.
>
> **Coach:** I'm sorry. He needs to be in school on time if
> he wants to play.
>
> **No Show's Dad:** This is just not acceptable.

Coach: I'm sorry. That's the rule.

No Show's Dad: I'm going to the principal.

Coach: You need to do what you think is right.

Over the years I've seen children taken out of school to get their ears pierced, to take care of siblings, to go shopping, to get their hair cut, to have lunch at a nice restaurant, to pick out a dog at the shelter, and to pick out a prom dress at the mall. Of course, to be fair, I've also seen kids come to school with earaches, fevers, and spots. Maybe it all evens out, but I doubt it.

It is difficult for the teacher to prevent absences when they occur with the full consent (or even encouragement) of the parent. Making it even more difficult for the teacher is that if she confronts the student about a suspicious absence, No Show's Dad will blithely supply a legitimate excuse for the child's not being there. "Getting Emily's ears pierced," for example, may suddenly become, "having a dentist appointment."

The best a teacher can do in these circumstances is to hold the child accountable for work missed, despite the absence. She should insist that the child make up assignments and call the parents to solicit their support. Should a parent fail to cooperate, I suggest that the teacher keep a log of those calls and the parent's response. Some parents may need to be reminded of a teacher's previous efforts when the report card comes out.

While chronic absenteeism is a problem at all levels, it is particularly a problem at the elementary level when kids are learning basic skills. At the elementary level, parents can sometimes be overprotective, keeping a child home if she complains of the mildest of upset tummies. At the high school level, on the other hand, parents are sometimes underprotective, turning their heads to ignore frequent truancy.

While chronic absenteeism is a problem at all levels, it is particularly a problem at the elementary level when kids are learning basic skills.

When a child is chronically absent for no legitimate reason, some parents will look for other excuses for the child's lack of progress:

Parent: I'd like you to refer my child for testing. I think he has a learning disability.

Teacher: I can do that, but he's missed so many days this year that it will be hard to get a clear assessment.

Parent: He just hasn't made the progress he should.

Teacher: He's missed 45 days. Perhaps the problem is attendance.

Parent: Or maybe he's got a learning disability.

Teacher: Maybe, but I haven't seen any evidence of that. I'd like to see how he does when he's here every day. I think that would make a huge difference.

Parent: I know my rights. I want my child tested.

Teacher: I'll have the school psychologist mail you the consent forms.

When a child is chronically absent for no legitimate reason, some parents will look for other excuses for the child's lack of progress.

This area is a delicate one for teachers. Federal law gives parents the right to have their child tested, and the teacher certainly doesn't want to be seen as an obstacle in this regard. There is also a real possibility that, although the teacher doesn't recognize a disability, it may still exist.

Still, it *is* hard to guess how a child would have progressed if he had actually been in school. As long as you respect the parent's rights, it doesn't hurt to raise the question of the child's attendance as being part of the problem.

It's tough for a teacher to change parents' attitudes toward attendance. That doesn't mean you should stop trying:

Teacher: I'm worried about Patrick's attendance. He really needs to be here.

Parent: Well, he's had a little cold.

Teacher: It's going around, I know. But he missed some
   important instruction. He really needs to be here.

Parent: I'll try to help him catch up.

Teacher: That's good, but he really needs to be here.

It's the old broken record technique: He really needs to be here.
He really needs to be here. He really needs to be here.

When a parent is honest about a child's absence, it usually makes
things a lot easier—unless he thinks that honesty gives the child a free
pass:

Parent: I admit that Bobby skipped school last Friday
   for opening day at the ballpark.

Principal: I appreciate your honesty.

Parent: Well, unlike some parents, I'm not going to lie
   and say he had a dentist appointment or something
   like that.

Principal: As I said, I appreciate that.

Parent: So I don't think he should have a penalty.

Principal: Well, he still skipped school. He'll have to
   make up the time.

Parent: Other kids who were there said they were sick
   and they don't have a penalty. This is what we get for
   being honest!

It's a dilemma. You want to reward honesty, but you
also know that the reason being honest is laudable is
that the person is willing to take the consequences.
After all, if all a person had to do to escape punish-
ment was to "fess up," our prisons would be empty.

However, the parent is not going to want to debate
philosophy. The best course of action is generally to _____
try to find some kind of reasonable compromise:

Parent: The kids who lied don't get a penalty. This isn't
fair.

Teacher: I understand how you could feel that way.
Your son tells the truth and gets a penalty while
other kids get off scot-free. But he did skip. How
about if he stays after school for two afternoons
instead of three to make up the time?

Parent: Well, I'm not happy about it, but I guess it will
have to work.

*A welcoming
attitude on the
teacher's part
is particularly
important for
some unfortunate
kids who have
had to move
many times
during their
school years.*

Despite all the negative consequences of missing school, teachers
really have little control over attendance. We can encourage kids to
come to school, and we can talk to their parents and try to impress
upon them how important regular attendance is to the child's success. In the end, however, we can't control what the parent does
unless the absences become excessive enough to turn the problem
over to the legal authorities.

What you can do, however, as teaching professionals, is this:
when the child who is chronically absent finally does show up at
school, welcome him with open arms. You may be annoyed and frus-
trated that he has been absent for no real reason; after all, the absence
creates work for you, he doesn't have the materials, he isn't up to
speed, etc. However, giving the student a hard time only exacerbates
the problem. Why would he want to come back if it's going to be
unpleasant? So show him all the good things he's missing at school!

A welcoming attitude on the teacher's part is particularly important for some unfortunate kids who, through no fault of their own,
have had to move many times during their school years. I have
known children who have been in four or five schools before they get
to middle school. One family I knew enrolled the children every fall,
then went south for the winter and enrolled them in school there. In

the spring the family returned to the North and re-enrolled the children in the original school. Needless to say, few kids can handle with aplomb that kind of peripatetic life, so don't add to the problem. When they're in your classroom, even if it is just a pit stop, make it a warm and safe experience.

Parents who take kids out of school when they don't really have to send the message that school isn't as important as teachers would have them believe. We need to help them remember that 50% of success in life is showing up. The remaining 50% is effort. We need to work at making kids want to come to school because they don't want to miss anything, and we need to tell parents over and over what their child won't get to do or see or read or participate in when he isn't at school. One way we can do that is to communicate frequently with parents of absent children either by phone or weekly updates. It's a little additional effort, but it may pay off for the child.

Here are some ideas to keep in mind when dealing with No Show's Dad:

When they're in your classroom, even if it is just a pit stop, make it a warm and safe experience.

- If he asks for his child's work ahead of time, give him what you can and suggest how he might tutor the child while he is away.

- Do everything you can to educate No Show's Dad about how much the child misses when he's not in school.

- If attendance in school is required for participation in an extracurricular activity, stay the course. No Show's Dad needs to know that classroom attendance is a prerequisite for other activities.

- Point out how chronic absenteeism can negatively affect a child's progress, but be prepared to assist the parent who wants a referral for psychological or other testing.

- When a chronically absent child does appear, make her feel welcome and part of the class. Showing annoyance or ignoring the child only reinforces reasons not to come to school.

Of course, the most important thing you can do to encourage students to come to school is to make your classroom inviting and your lessons interesting and challenging. You can't *make* students come to school, but you can help make it a place where they feel wanted and welcome.

HELICOPTER MOM

True story: Several years ago a big football game was scheduled between two long-standing rivals. Not only was it Senior Night for the home team, but the outcome of the game would decide the league championship. Unfortunately, it had been raining for days, and the home team's football field had turned into a shallow lake. The opponents offered the use of their field, which had better drainage and was in better shape, but the home team's superintendent was loath to lose the home field advantage.

Instead, the superintendent, a former military man, called in a favor from a nearby army base. That afternoon a couple of helicopters arrived and hovered low over the field, the chopper blades whisking the standing water away from the ball field. The game was played, the home team won, and the superintendent and his helicopters became the stuff of local legend. It was glorious.

"Glorious" is not the word I would use to describe another kind of helicopter—the parent who hovers constantly, ready to whisk away any problem or inconvenience that might befall her child. The Helicopter Mom is heavily invested in every facet of her child's school day. Here's a typical conversation:

Helicopter Mom: Sorry to call you so late, Mrs. Baker,
but we're not sure if Ian's homework is page 37, the
odd problems, or page 36, the even problems.

Teacher: What? It's 11:00 at night!

*Helicopter
Mom begins
hovering when
her child is in
kindergarten
and never
lets up.*

Helicopter Mom begins hovering when her child is in kindergarten and never lets up. Sometimes she actually starts much earlier,
preschool or even sooner, hovering over the crib with flash cards
while Baby Einstein videos tinkle Mozart in the background.

She is always at her child's beck and call, just a child's cell phone
call away, ready to intervene at any moment. Miss the bus on Monday?
Mom will drive you to school. Miss the bus on Tuesday, Wednesday,
Thursday and Friday? Hop in the car. Forget your violin? Mom will
deliver it to the main office before orchestra meets. Lose your gym
shoes? Mom will get you another pair tonight. Fail the math test? It
probably wasn't fair. Talk back to the teacher? You didn't really mean it.

Helicopter Mom spends a lot of time at the school or on the
phone. She questions the teacher about his grading practices. She
challenges the pronunciation of words at the spelling bee. She inter-
rogates the principal about the dress code. She wonders whether
children should go outside for recess if the temperature drops. She
calls at the first snowflake to see if school is going to close early. She
yells at the referee. She challenges the superintendent about graduation honors. Eventually, she fills out her child's college applications
and probably drafts his college essay, too. It doesn't take long for the
child to get the lay of the land:

Teacher: Mark, that language is not acceptable in my
classroom. I'll see you after school.

Mark: I need to call my mom first to see if she'll let me stay.

Or:

Teacher: Christine, your answer is right, but you didn't show your work.

Christine: My mom helped me on my homework last night. She said it's okay not to show my work if I could do it in my head.

Teacher: It's great that your mom helped you, but I need to see the work.

Christine: My mom said it didn't matter.

Or:

Helicopter Mom: Alan has soccer practice every night after school, so he's not going to get his health project in until next Monday.

Teacher: The projects are due on Friday.

Helicopter Mom: I don't want Alan getting stressed out over this.

Teacher: Well, I don't either, but the students have had over a week to complete this project.

Helicopter Mom: Don't worry. He'll have it on Monday.

Teacher: I'm not worried. But if it's handed in past the due date, he'll lose points.

Helicopter Mom: I just don't think that's fair.

Teacher: I'm sorry. But I need to apply the grading procedures equally to all my students.

Helicopter Mom: It's too bad you can't be more flexible.

Helicopter Mom has a very hard time letting her child take responsibility for his actions.

Helicopter Mom has a very hard time letting her child take responsibility for his actions:

Helicopter Mom: I brought this for Mark's lunch.

Secretary: I think he has in-school suspension today.

Helicopter Mom: I know that. I thought a
McDonald's Happy Meal would cheer him up.

There is a difference, of course, between parents who are simply interested and involved in their child's school and parents who need to know everything that's going on so that they can shepherd their child through each day and every class, protecting her from any real responsibility. Helicopter Mom is likely to make demands on the teacher, rather than on her child:

Teacher: Amy is not handing in all of her homework.
Helicopter Mom: I'd like you to send home a daily
report about what she's turned in and what she still
needs to do.
Teacher: I have 135 students. I can't promise to do that.
Helicopter Mom: I would think that would be part of
your job.

It isn't easy for the teacher to put responsibility back on the student, but that's where it belongs.

It isn't easy for the teacher to put responsibility back on the student, but that's where it belongs:

Teacher: With 135 students, I can't promise you that
I'd be able to send home a daily report.
Helicopter Mom: How am I supposed to know if Amy
does her work then?
Teacher: You could ask Amy when she gets home to
show you her homework.
Parent: She always says she's already done it.
Teacher: How about if she writes down the assignment
every day in her plan book and I'll initial it? You can
check when she gets home to see what her assignment is.
Helicopter Mom: How will that help?
Teacher: Well, I suggest that along with her plan book,

you insist that she bring her math book home every day. You can check the assignment and ask her to show you her work.

A favorite Helicopter Mom ploy to help a child avoid consequences is to insist that the child didn't know what was expected. He didn't know when the paper was due. He didn't know he needed to use three sources for the research. He didn't know he needed a title page. He didn't know he needed to do his own work. He didn't know the project was half of his final grade. All of these excuses will make the teacher want to ask what the child *does* know, besides how to manipulate his mother.

Often, what Helicopter Mom really wants to show is that every problem is really the teacher's fault because he didn't tell the child. Here's an all too common conversation:

Helicopter Mom: Alana didn't know the test was going to be Friday.

Teacher: I reminded students daily and it was on the board all week.

Helicopter Mom: She doesn't always look at the board.

Teacher: I sent the information home in my weekly update.

Helicopter Mom: She must have forgotten to give it to me.

Teacher: Well, that's unfortunate, but there isn't much more I can do besides telephone you every day right after class.

Helicopter Mom: That would be great!

Teacher: (*startled*) I'm joking.

Oops. The teacher forgot the "no sarcasm" rule, but you can see how that could happen.

Other excuses Helicopter Mom uses for her child is that the work is too hard, the assignments too long, or the test too difficult. The teacher needs to reassure her that he knows the child and that he is confident that the child is capable of doing what is assigned. The teacher should add that he has the same expectations of all the other students as well. Here is an example of one way to handle Helicopter Mom:

On the other end of the spectrum, some Helicopter Moms fret over things that most other parents don't even notice, and as a consequence, can put a great deal of pressure on their kids.

Helicopter Mom: I really think that 25 pages of reading a night are too much.

Teacher: Students have time to begin in class.

Helicopter Mom: Brad just can't stay awake to finish it. Besides, he needs to have a little time to relax and play video games.

Teacher: Brad is a bright boy. He can do this. Of course I expect the same from him as from other students.

Helicopter Mom: I just don't want him to become discouraged with school.

Teacher: He's a pretty positive kid. And I know that kids need to have time to relax and do something else besides schoolwork. It's not easy to balance everything. But maybe he can play video games after he does his reading—sort of as a reward.

Helicopter Mom: I don't see that as a reward. He deserves to have some downtime.

Teacher: How many pages a night do you think Brad can read?

Helicopter Mom: I have no idea. Not 25.

Teacher: How about if you monitor his reading for a week. Let me know what he can accomplish in half an hour. We have quite a bit of reading to get

through this semester, and students need to organize
their time to stay on top of it.

On the other end of the spectrum, some Helicopter Moms fret
over things that most other parents don't even notice, and as a consequence, can put a great deal of pressure on their kids:

Helicopter Mom: I see Madeline's math grade
dropped three points.

Teacher: She still has a 94 in math.

Helicopter Mom: What did she miss?

Teacher: Actually, I'm not really sure. There were a lot of
assignments and quizzes over the last marking period.

Helicopter Mom: Can she do something for extra credit?

Teacher: She got a 94!

Helicopter Mom: Maybe we should get her a tutor.

Teacher: Maybe you should get a life.

Well, by now you know the teacher shouldn't really say that. He
should say something like this, instead:

Teacher: Let's wait and see how she does over the next
few weeks. Madeline's an excellent student and a lot
of fun to teach. Grades tend to fluctuate a little for
all students, so I really think she'll be fine. If not, I'll
let you know.

Helicopter Mom: Okay. But please call me as soon as
there's a problem.

Besides an abiding interest in her own child's progress, Helicopter
Mom sometimes has a similar interest in the progress of other students. Protecting her own child means making sure that no other
child has an unfair advantage. In conversations like this one, it is
important not to acknowledge her point:

*Besides an abiding
interest in her own
child's progress,
Helicopter Mom
sometimes has a
similar interest
in the progress of
other students.*

Helicopter Mom: My daughter's written work is a lot better than Oren's.

Teacher: I have a policy not to talk about other children.

Helicopter Mom: Well, I'm just saying that Nan should get the writing award at sixth grade graduation. I've seen Oren's work, and I know that Nan's is better.

Teacher: Nan is a very good writer.

Helicopter Mom:: I'd say the best in the class.

Teacher: She is very good—as are several of the other students.

Here's another example:

Helicopter Mom: I see Isabel got a perfect attendance award. Why didn't my Lewis get one?

Teacher: Ahhh...Lewis didn't have perfect attendance.

Helicopter Mom: He was only absent twice this year.

Teacher: Well, perfect means being here every day.

Helicopter Mom: I know for a fact that Isabel's mother brings her to school even when she's sick. Lewis was out two days because he caught a cold from her.

Teacher: Really, there's no way of knowing exactly who gives whom a cold.

Helicopter Mom: I saw Isabel in the nurses' office, coughing and sneezing when I came to pick up Lewis one day.

Teacher: Really, I can't comment on that. I'm sorry, but perfect attendance means just that. The child has to be here every day.

Helicopter Mom: Well, I just think it's not fair.

If it is not your policy not to talk about other students, it should be.

If it is not your policy not to talk about other students, it should be. Professional ethics demand that you respect the privacy of all of your students. Helicopter Mom can be insistent, and you have to adhere to your ethical position. Here's one approach:

> **Helicopter Mom:** Beth says that the reason she did poorly on the test is that you spend all your time helping Larry. Isn't he one of those "special" kids?
>
> **Teacher:** I'm sorry. I can't talk about other students.
>
> **Helicopter Mom:** Well, I don't know why those kids are in regular classes. It takes the teacher's time away from the other students.
>
> **Teacher:** Really, I just don't talk about other students.
>
> **Helicopter Mom:** It doesn't seem fair to the rest of the kids.
>
> **Teacher:** Beth didn't do well on the test because she missed a couple of days and didn't come in for extra help.
>
> **Helicopter Mom:** Well, if you weren't so busy with those special kids, you could have helped her in class.
>
> **Teacher:** All kids are special.

You get the picture. Refuse to be drawn into any comparison between or among your students.

Helicopter Mom often loves to volunteer at school. While having parent volunteers usually works out wonderfully for both the parent and the school, teachers need to be alert when Helicopter Mom is involved. She may find it difficult not to interfere on her child's behalf—as in chastising a first grader who won't sit next to her child at lunch. Or she may not respect another child's right to privacy, telling tales out of school about a child who may have had a problem of some sort in school that day.

If you have parent volunteers in your classroom, never, never allow them to grade papers or enter information

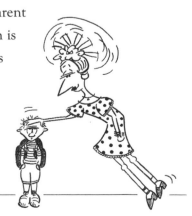

into a grade book or other kind of record. Doing so compromises the confidentiality of your classroom. And never share personal information about another child in your classroom with a parent volunteer.

In dealing with Helicopter Mom, the best defense is a good offense. Keep her informed of her child's progress, by phone, e-mail, snail mail or conference. Many schools today even have online programs that allow parents 24-hour access to their child's grades and assignments. Regular communication makes it hard for a student or her parents to claim ignorance. By the same token, failing to inform a parent of a problem will indeed make it your problem—and rightly so. Keeping parents informed when their child is not being successful is part of our professional duty.

In dealing with Helicopter Mom, the best defense is a good offense.

Helicopter Mom can be trying to a teacher, but think of how trying she also must be to a child struggling to balance roots and wings. It is Helicopter Mom's lack of perspective that gets her into trouble. The teacher's job is to help establish and then maintain a sense of perspective for her.

Here are some strategies to remember when dealing with Helicopter Mom:

- Reassure her that her child is capable and can compete with the other students in the classroom.

- Communicate with her as clearly and frequently as possible.

- Insist that her child play by the same rules as all the other children.

- Keep to yourself confidential information about her child and other children.

- Rejoice that at least she cares about her child!

THE COMPETITOR

With the Competitor, every encounter with the teacher is a contest. She enters your classroom like a World Federation Wrestler climbing into the ring. She's already pumped up and eager to fight for what she wants. She makes it clear that if she gets her way, she wins and you lose. She approaches every situation as if it were a serious competition that will probably end in a smackdown. You will be the one lying flat out in the middle of the ring, unless you know how to handle her.

As teachers, we know that working with kids is not about winning and losing. We know that teaching is not about who's right. We know that working with parents should be a cooperative effort, not a competition. We struggle to remain professional, but a confrontational parent can press every one of our buttons. It isn't long before the idea of winning becomes pretty appealing to us as well. Here's a typical conversation:

Competitor: Your writing program isn't very effective.

Teacher: Why do you say that?

Competitor: I did a little research yesterday on the Internet.

Teacher: *(thinking)* And I did a little research in my five years of college.
 (aloud) So what did you find?

The Competitor does not like to be wrong.

Competitor: Here, I've printed it off for you. You can read it later. This study shows that kids can move more easily from printing to writing if you use the Gutenberg method.

Teacher: Thanks, I'll look it over.

Competitor: Great. I'll call you in a couple of days about changing the writing program.

Teacher: I don't think we'll be changing the writing program.

Competitor: We'll see...

Here's another example:

Competitor: In the last school we were in, the teachers and kids all made piñatas for the last day of class before the holidays.

Teacher: How nice.

Competitor: I want to do that here. It would be fun.

Teacher: It *would* be fun. Maybe we could do something like that next year.

Competitor: There's no reason not to do it this year.

Teacher: Actually, it's only two weeks until vacation and we have other things planned.

Competitor: I'll get some mothers to help. Kids need to have fun in school.

Teacher: I agree—about the fun. But we won't have time for that this year.

Competitor: I'm sure you can find just an hour for fun. Let's plan on it.

Teacher: Every day is fun. *(thinking)* Except for today.

The Competitor does not like to be wrong. She also doesn't like for you to be right. She will not hesitate to point out the error of your ways:

Competitor: I rechecked Michael's math test and you
graded one of the problems wrong.

Teacher: I did?

Competitor: Yes. He had it right and you marked it
wrong.

Teacher:: Let me see. Hmm. Yes, I think I did miss one.

Competitor: So you were wrong, not Michael.

The Competitors do not like to admit mistakes themselves. If
they have not been successful with their child in some areas, they
may not want you to be either because it makes them look bad.

It can't be a competition if you refuse to compete.

Teacher: Waldo needs to stay with me after school to
make up work he didn't do.

Competitor: He'll never do that.

Teacher: Then he'll fail.

Competitor: You're letting him fail.

Teacher: I'm giving him the opportunity to do the work.

Competitor: He won't stay.

Teacher: You can't make him stay?

Competitor: You can't either.

These kinds of exchanges can be maddening. However, you need
to keep in mind that it can't be a competition if you refuse to compete:

Teacher: Waldo needs to stay with me after school to
make up work he didn't do.

Competitor: He'll never do that.

Teacher: Can you help me get him to stay?

Competitor: Look, he's a big kid now. He makes his
own decisions.

Teacher: Maybe you would have more success making
him stay than I would.

*The Competitor
is taken off
guard when you
refuse to play
the win-lose
game.*

Competitor: Me?

Teacher: Well, I can't seem to do it. You're his dad. I'll
bet you would have more success with Waldo than
his teacher would.

Competitor: I doubt if he'll listen to me, either.

Teacher: Well, maybe I can get him to make up some
work during his lunch or study hall.

Competitor: Maybe. You could try it. And I can tell
him that he should work with you during study hall.

Note what the teacher has done. He doesn't say what he's
tempted to say, which is "Okay, forget it. If you don't care, why
should I?" Instead of pushing against the parent, the teacher pulls
him over to his side.

The Competitor is taken off guard when you refuse to play the
win-lose game. Admittedly, it often isn't easy to think win-win with
her. She may challenge you in the classroom or on the phone or via
your e-mail, trying your patience and testing your cool. It is helpful to
remember, however, that the hostility aimed at you is sometimes a
result of her own frustrations with the child. This misdirected frustra-
tion can come across as something else—bravado, disrespect, or anger
towards the teacher.

Here is an example of a conversation that is going nowhere fast:

Competitor: Why is my son staying in when all the
other kids go out for recess?

Teacher: Kids who haven't finished their work need to
finish it before they can go out.

Competitor: I want him outside with the other kids.

Teacher: That's not the rule in third grade. Jimmy
needs to learn to finish his work.

Competitor: I do not want him staying in. He needs
to go out and play with everyone else.

Teacher: He can go out when he finishes his work.

Clearly, if the teacher lets Jimmy go out without finishing his
work, he loses. The teacher, that is. Well, Jimmy does, too. So how
do you keep the parent from "winning"?

Think win-win. What does the parent really want? First of all, he
probably doesn't want his child to be stigmatized or embarrassed by
being the only one stuck inside the classroom on a glorious fall afternoon. In truth, no parent would want that—nor would you if it were
your child. It is important to realize that what the parent really wants
is for his kid to do his work like all the other kids. Going outside is
unlikely to be the real issue. Sometimes a teacher needs to hear what
isn't being said.

In a case like this, it is probably a good idea for the teacher to figure
out another plan to help Jimmy get his work done—one that involves
the parent's help. Otherwise, the parent will focus on the side issue
(playtime) instead of the main issue (Jimmy's failure to do his work).

Teacher: I don't like to see kids miss playtime, especially
Jimmy. He needs to work off some of that energy.
But there's only so much time in the school day and
you know how Jimmy procrastinates. Do you have
any suggestions to help him get his work done?

Competitor: Not really. You're the teacher.

Teacher: When he doesn't get his work done, he falls
behind in class. Third grade is an important year.
I worry about his progress in reading comprehension
and I know you do, too.

Competitor: I do worry about that. But he still
needs his playtime.

Teacher: How about a compromise? He gets ten minutes of playtime after ten minutes of homework.

Competitor: Well, I guess we could start there.

Of course, this particular solution won't work for all cases. The point is simply that if there is going to be any kind of reasonable solution, it will probably fall to the teacher to work out some kind of compromise. If the teacher can acknowledge some validity in a parent's concern, she can open a dialogue that at least has a chance of ending with a positive outcome.

Here's another example of a conversation with the Competitor:

Competitor: Alysha is being bullied by Natalie and it needs to stop immediately!

Teacher: I thought Alysha and Natalie were best friends.

Competitor: They were. But since a new girl moved here, they're not anymore. You should know that.

Teacher: What does the bullying look like?

Competitor: They don't talk to her and whisper about her. It needs to stop! This is happening in your classroom.

Teacher: I'll talk to them.

Competitor: Well, I'm holding you accountable. If it doesn't stop, I'll go to the principal.

Teacher: You need to do what you think is right. But just so you know, I realize that there is nothing more painful in 7th grade than the way girls sometimes treat one another. I'll work on it.

Competitor: I just hate to see Alysha so unhappy.

Teacher: We need to find a way to solve this problem.

Finding a solution to the problem, however, often requires that the teacher ignore all of the implied criticisms the parent brings to

If the teacher can acknowledge some validity in a parent's concern, she can open a dialogue that at least has a chance of ending with a positive outcome.

the conversation, which is not an easy task. Again, if you can figure out what the parent really wants (and it's not always what the parent says), you may be able to find a way to work through the situation so that everyone wins, including the child.

Sometimes, however, what the parent says is exactly what she wants—but she just can't have it. Here's an example of when a teacher needs to hold her ground:

> **Competitor:** When you call on Mary and she doesn't
>   know the answer, it embarrasses her. So I want you
>   to stop calling on her.
> **Teacher:** Mary always has the option to pass.
> **Competitor:** Then other kids will still think she doesn't
>   know the answer.
> **Teacher:** Other kids pass too.
> **Competitor:** I'm telling you: I don't want you to call
>   on her anymore.
> **Teacher:** I'm sorry. That's part of the learning process
>   and a quick way for me to find out if Mary under-
>   stands the material. I will be calling on her.
> **Competitor:** Then I guess I'll have to talk to the principal.
> **Teacher:** Bring it on.

Okay, by now you know that's just a little joke. You should not say, "Bring it on." You should say, "Go for it."

No, not really. What you should really say (as we've noted before) is, "You need to do what you think is right."

Let's recap some of the suggestions for dealing with the Competitor:

- Refuse to be drawn into a competition that is likely to produce a winner and loser.

If you can figure out what the parent really wants, you may be able to find a way to work through the situation so that everyone wins, including the child.

- Think win-win. How can you find a workable compromise? Look for common ground.

- Listen to what the parent is *not* saying. Ignore, if possible, the implied criticisms and focus on the real issue.

- Encourage the parent with completely unreasonable demands to take them to the principal.

When you have managed to deal successfully with the Competitor, feel free to close your door, raise both arms, and do a victory lap around the desks.

WHO'S THE FAIREST OF THEM ALL?

One year an eighth grade boy who was a real "itch" complained to me about another teacher. "She always yells at me," he said.

"Mark," I chided him, "I yell at you, too."

"Yeah," he said, "but you yell at all of us. Not just me."

Every teacher has, at one time or another, a student who drives her to distraction. Mark was one of those kids. I was a little anxious about meeting his parents, but they seemed pleasant enough when they arrived in my classroom.

I began my litany of Mark's offenses: he didn't do his homework, he wasn't always on time for class, he spoke without raising his hand, he talked to other students when I was talking. His parents shook their heads in commiseration. "Yes, he's a handful," his dad agreed. "But he's a good boy. And you're his favorite teacher."

"What?" I said. "I'm his favorite teacher? That's impossible! I'm on that boy's case from the beginning of class to the end!"

"Well," said his dad, "he says you're tough, but you're tough on everyone."

Frankly, I wasn't sure whether to take this as a compliment or not. But when I thought about it, I remembered that kids have a rich, innate sense of what is fair and what is not. It turns out that Mark was okay with my yelling at him because he wasn't the only one and because he knew it meant I cared about what he did. He was pretty sure I liked him, even if I wasn't always happy with his behavior, which he admitted, with typical eighth grade candor, wasn't always exemplary. (Just for the record, I use "yell" in the sense of speaking loudly but sweetly!)

Good teaching demands fairness. This is an important point to remember not only from a professional ethics standpoint, but also from the standpoint of dealing with your students' parents. Difficult parents can be confrontational and demanding. If a teacher has actually been unfair to their child, they can be even more confrontational and demanding—and also right.

Good teaching demands fairness.

We need to make every effort to treat all children the way we would want our own child's teacher to treat her. Remember that every parent wants to know if his child is just another student to you, or whether you really know him. Parents want to know if they can count on you to treat their child fairly, even kindly. They hope that you see in their son or daughter all the special things that they do.

If you are a parent as well as a teacher, you know exactly what I mean. If you're not a parent, think of a child you love—a niece or nephew, the kid next door, or even yourself as a child. Be the kind of teacher you wanted to have when you were a kid.

And that is the hard part: in the real world of teaching, you will not like all children equally. After all, you don't like all adults equally, do you? The trick is that no one should ever be able to guess which child you like and which child you just can't warm up to. It is important to particularly monitor your behavior with kids you may find less than appealing, to be sure that you treat all children equally.

If you are always fair, you may, on occasion, even find yourself with an opportunity to help a student whose behavior isn't particularly charming:

Charlie: You're the Honor Society advisor. So how come I didn't get in?

Ms. Anderson: Sit down, Charlie. Let's talk. Do you
have any thoughts yourself?

Charlie: Teachers don't like me.

The temptation for Ms. Anderson would be to say the following:

Ms. Anderson: Well, duh! You're smart, but you're rude
and lazy. Honor Society is about more than grades!

Instead, she acts like the professional she is—and that we should
all hope to be:

Charlie: Teachers don't like me.

Ms. Anderson: Why do you say that?

Charlie: I don't know. They just don't.

Ms. Anderson: Can you give me an example of what
you mean?

Charlie: Well, like Ms. Banks, my English teacher.

Ms. Anderson: Why would Ms. Banks not like you?

Charlie: I dunno. Well, there was that time I told her
to f-off.

Ms. Anderson: Well, duh!

No, she doesn't really say that. She's a professional. She says this:

Ms. Anderson: Can you see how that might change
how she thinks of you?

Charlie: Yeah.

Ms. Anderson: So what do you think you can do about it?

Charlie: Well, I guess I could watch what I say to her.
She just makes me so mad sometimes!

While this brief conversation won't change Charlie overnight, his
teacher's willingness to talk to him about a real problem is a step in the

*And that is
the hard part:
in the real world
of teaching, you
will not like all
children equally*

right direction. We need to remember that for some kids, it's the adult guidance they get in school that makes a difference in their lives.

Students recognize when they themselves are not treated fairly. They also recognize when other students are not treated fairly. I have known teachers who thought they would ingratiate themselves with their students by making jokes at another student's expense. While some kids laughed, the teacher lost respect in their eyes—because kids not only understand fairness; they also understand power. When a teacher picks on a student just because he can do so with impunity, it offends the students' sense of what's right. Kids may pick on one another themselves, but it's not the same thing when the teacher does it.

Kids may pick on one another themselves, but it's not the same thing when the teacher does it.

Why spend so much time on fairness? Here's why: stuff happens in schools that we can't control. Therefore, it is very important to control what we can. Remember Helicopter Mom? We can't always predict what will make her decide to swoop in and land on us. But we can guarantee that she will be revving up her engines if you let one child re-take a poor test but deny that privilege to her son. If you think Ms. "Quit Picking on My Kid!" is unreasonable, wait until you ignore foul language from one kid and remove her child from class for the same offense. And you really don't want to have to face the Intimidator after you've humiliated his child by pointing out to his classmates how he can't even tie his shoes.

We know that there's just no pleasing some people. However, we can conduct ourselves in a way that minimizes encounters with difficult parents by perfecting our skills, thinking before we act, and fine-tuning our sense of fairness in our interactions with our students.

As teachers, we all need to be critical of our own work. If not, others will do the criticizing for us.

TIPS FOR EFFECTIVE PARENT CONFERENCES

So it's parent-teacher conference time again, and you are completely prepared. You know that some parents will be intimidated or annoyed if you sit behind your desk while they sit like students in front of you. Therefore, you will meet with them at a table, or perhaps you will all be seated at student desks. You want to show that you are all on the same side.

You have organized examples of each student's work, as well as test results, in folders that you can immediately put your hands on. You may also have at your fingertips printed materials that explain your reading program or an upcoming project or requirements for a state test.

You plan to start each conference on time and end promptly so that parents don't get backed up waiting to see you. You know which parents don't have the same surname as their child. You are dressed professionally, and you are not drinking coffee or a soda or anything else that parents will not have access to.

Before you rise to greet your first parent and shake his or her hand, you remember what we said at the outset: All parents want to be reassured that you really know their child, that he or she is not just another student to you, and that you will do your best to help him or her learn. Parents may also want to know how their child is doing in comparison to other students; that is, is their child at the top of the class, somewhere in the middle, or lagging behind? If he isn't making adequate progress, is he getting the extra help he needs? Also, you will want to keep in mind that, particularly at the elementary and middle school level, parents want to know how their child gets along with other children.

In 98% of the meetings, both you and the parents will actually have an enjoyable time and will feel as if you are working together for the benefit of the child.

Then there is the other 2%. Luckily, you will have reviewed some of the ideas and strategies we have talked about in this book, so you can go in with a plan for dealing with difficult parents. Some reminders:

- Insist on specifics if a parent criticizes something he thinks you have done—or not done. What happened? When? Where? Who was involved? How much homework is too much? What specifically was "unfair" about the test? What in particular is objectionable about the reading assignment?

- Remember that a parent can speak for her child only. Keep the conversation focused on that child, not on anyone else's child.

- Think ahead. Conference time can be a good time to let parents know what projects, books, or assignments you may have in mind for the future. It is easier to

In 98% of the meetings, both you and the parents will actually have an enjoyable time and feel as if you are working together for the benefit of the child.

garner support if parents know what will be expected of their child.

• Be a broken record. When parents want to wander off the topic, stay fixated on the issue at hand:

Teacher: Jack's frequent absences are affecting his work.
Parent: He spent last week at his dad's house.
Teacher: He's missed some important instruction.
Parent: His father lets him do what he wants.
Teacher: It's hard for him to get caught up when he's out so much.
Parent: His father lets him stay up too late and then he can't get up the next day.
Teacher: I'm hopeful that his attendance will improve because it's going to affect his later work as well.

• Refuse to be intimidated. You are a trained professional who understands classroom management and child behavior. Remember that if a parent becomes abusive or threatening, it's time to end the conference:

Parent: I expect to see an improvement in Terry's grade in Spanish.
Teacher: Part of Terry's grade is participation in class. When he doesn't do the homework, he's not prepared to participate.
Parent: That is the stupidest idea I've ever heard! How can you grade participation?
Teacher: Students should be prepared to respond in Spanish to questions in class.
Parent: This isn't the only course he has. But it's

*Remember
that if a parent
becomes abusive
or threatening,
it's time to end
the conference.*

119

certainly the most useless course. And you're the
most useless teacher.

Teacher: *(standing)* This conference is over.

- Never, ever use sarcasm when speaking to parents.
  Sarcasm only inflames an already volatile situation and
  diminishes you as a professional, as in this example:

*Never, ever
use sarcasm
when speaking
to parents.*

Parent: This is a useless class and you're a useless teacher.
Teacher: Well, you ought to know about useless.
Parent: *(climbing over the desk)* What?

- Don't respond in kind to a hostile parent. Instead,
  remember that hostile parents can sometimes be
  mollified if you can ignore the hostility and respond
  with a courtesy you may not actually feel:

Parent: Jackie just can't get all the work done that you
assign. It's too much to expect from sixth graders!
Teacher: Help me understand what she finds so difficult.

- Refuse to acknowledge anonymous complaints.

Parent: I know for a fact that you favor the girls in your
class.
Teacher: How would you know that?
Parent: I have my sources.
Teacher: Really, I can't respond to that.
Parent: Well, the kids know it. Even the girls say you
favor them.
Teacher: Kids say a lot of things. Let's talk about
Connor's report card.

- Stay the course. Some things are not negotiable:

Parent: Okay, Beth admits she cheated on the test. But I don't see why she can't just take it over.

Teacher: She will get a zero for the test.

Parent: She admits she was wrong.

Teacher: That's a good thing. However, there is a penalty for cheating.

Parent: Why can't she just take it again?

Teacher: She is familiar with the test. I am offering that she do a paper instead to make up for the zero.

Parent: That isn't fair. No one else has to do a paper.

Teacher: No one else cheated on the test.

Parent: She's not going to do it.

Teacher: That's her choice. But the zero then stands.

• Encourage parents to make sure their children come to school, and on time. Unfortunately, parents of absentee kids are frequently no shows themselves at conferences, so a phone call may be required. While the call may not work miracles, not bothering to call certainly has no chance of success. When you call, try to be as positive as possible:

Teacher: I missed you at parent conferences last night.

Parent: I had to work.

Teacher: Well, I'm glad I caught you at home this morning. Trisha is doing pretty well in school, but I'm worried about her tardiness.

Parent: It's not easy getting her up.

Teacher: I understand, but she's missing out on a lot.

Parent: I know. I tell her that.

Teacher: I hope you can get her to school on time.

Parent: Well, I'll try.

- Show parents how you are helping students build confidence through accomplishment. Focus first on what the child is able to do and how you plan to build upon the skills she already has. A good way of doing this is to contrast the student's work at the beginning of the year with where she is today:

Teacher: Here's a sample of Gretchen's writing last September. Look at what she can do now!

Or:

Teacher: Matthew has his addition and subtraction facts down pretty well, but he needs to work on multiplication.

Be sensitive to parents' hopes and dreams for their child, but be direct enough so that parents are not confused about your message.

- Walk like you mean it. In other words, know what you're going to say before the conference so you can say it with conviction. Practice can be helpful, particularly if the conference involves giving parents information they may not want to hear. Be sensitive to parents' hopes and dreams for their child, but be direct enough so that parents are not confused about your message:

Teacher: Steve has made progress in reading, but he's still not where he needs to be.

Parent: What does that mean?

Teacher: He's about a year below grade level. That's why he has an extra reading class each day.

- Don't deny. Clarify:

Parent: You never call on Ben.
Teacher: Never?
Parent: Not very often.
Teacher: How many times a week?
Parent: I have no idea.
Teacher: I may not get to every student every day, but I
try to get to as many as possible. Maybe you could
ask Ben how often he thinks I should call on him.

- Be sure you can justify your classroom rules or procedures as important for students rather than just for
your own convenience.

Parent: Can Steve stay with you on Tuesdays to work
on his multiplication tables?
Teacher: I usually drink coffee and grade papers in the
faculty room on Tuesdays.

Just wanted to see if you were still paying attention! Of course,
you don't say that. Here's what you say instead:

Teacher: I'll be here.

*Try not to take
parent criticism
personally, even
when you're
pretty sure it is
meant that way.*

- Try not to take parent criticism personally, even when
you're pretty sure it is meant that way. Remember
that parents who are difficult to deal with probably
didn't start being difficult with you (unless you are a
preschool teacher). They probably won't stop with
you, either (unless you teach seniors in high school).

- Let parents vent. If you know that parents are upset
about something before a conference, it's often a good
idea to just let them talk. They won't hear anything

you say anyway until their issue is resolved. Don't interrupt except to ask clarifying questions:

Teacher: Thank you for coming in. I'm interested in hearing your concerns.

Parent: Well, it's about the play try-outs you had in class.

Teacher: Yes?

Parent: Rachel never gets a good part. She thought she was going to get to be Cinderella, but instead you picked Rebecca, who always gets those parts just because she's thin and blond. Rachel is just as good, maybe better, and last year when they did Peter Pan she ended up being the dog and Rebecca, as usual, got to be Wendy.

Teacher: I see.

Parent: She came home and cried and cried. She doesn't want to be an Ugly Stepsister. Rebecca's mother is always here at school helping out and I think that makes a big difference. I work full-time and can't be here.

Teacher: Okay. Is there more?

Parent: Well, I just think that things should be spread around. Rachel tries really hard and every time she loses out. Two years ago she had to be a tree when Rebecca got to be a wood sprite. It's just not fair.

Teacher: I see your point. Maybe we can find a part for Rachel in the next play that allows her to do a little more.

However this issue is resolved, it's clear that before Rachel's mom can talk about her daughter's progress in math, she needs to make it

Sometimes a teacher can learn a lot about a child (and maybe about herself) by just letting the parent vent.

clear that in the next play Rachel shouldn't have to be a bench while
Rebecca gets to be a trial lawyer. Sometimes a teacher can learn a lot
about a child (and maybe about herself) by just letting the parent
vent. Maybe the teacher has never thought about how something as
simple as a school play can impact a child's feelings about herself or
about school. Maybe the teacher needs to think about how parts are
assigned.

On the other hand, maybe the parent needs to know that Rachel
is so shy and anxious that when she has to do an oral report the
teacher worries that she'll faint and hit her head on the chalk tray.

- Be prepared to end a conference if a parent becomes
  personally insulting.

The great majority of parent conferences will be positive and useful. When they are not, you should have the strategies to make your
points clearly without exacerbating the situation. If the parent
becomes abusive, however, it's "Game over!"

WHEN NOTHING WORKS

At this point, we need to note that despite our best skills and efforts, some parents will simply refuse to be cooperative and work with the teacher for their child's benefit. Maybe their expectations for their child or for the teacher are unreasonable. Maybe their attitude toward school in general is negative. Maybe their lot in life is to be just plain ornery. Whatever the reason, a very, very small minority of parents will resist all of our attempts to come to an amicable resolution to the problems they perceive. When you have exhausted all of your strategies and maybe your patience, you may simply decide to put the cards on the table:

Teacher: Mr. Barton, I think we're at an impasse. I cannot in good conscience change Brian's grade. You will need to take this problem to the principal.

Or:

Teacher: Mrs. Wilcox, it seems that we cannot come to an agreement about what's best for your daughter. We may have to just live with the fact that this is the way I run my class. I know you're unhappy, but this is how I do it.

Or:

Teacher: Mr. Samson, you cannot call me at home. You
may call me at school and leave a message, and I will
get back to you as soon as I can. But I will not call
you more than once a week.

Or:

*You will have
made it clear
that there are
limits to what
any teaching
professional
should have
to tolerate.*

Teacher: I recognize that we don't agree. But Amanda
will have to be respectful in my class or she cannot
stay. And you cannot show up in my classroom every
time you disagree with my rules.

Or:

Teacher: Ms. Peterson, please be aware that from now
on I will not meet with you without the principal
present.

These tactics will not necessarily make a demanding parent less
demanding. However, you will have made it clear that there are limits
to what any teaching professional should have to tolerate. From this
point on the parent will have to deal with the administration. (Of
course, you will have kept the administration informed all along.)

From a district-wide perspective, the administration should insist
on a "chain of command" approach to handling garden variety parent
complaints: first teacher, then principal, then various supervisors,
then superintendent, then board of education. This philosophy can
be shared with parents in newsletters and school handbooks, and
school administrators can help by insisting that parents follow the
chain of command with common problems. While the teacher can't
control how the district operates in this regard, she can frequently

remind parents—in notes home, in phone calls, or in conferences—that if there is a problem, she wants to hear about it first.

Of course, there are circumstances that demand the principal's or even superintendent's immediate attention—serious incidents that involve a child's safety or well being. There are, unfortunately, occasions where a parent needs to move swiftly to the top to rectify a situation or remove their child from harm's way. But the usual kinds of classroom complaints that parents have—grades, homework, tests, assignments, behavior, attendance, etc.—should first be addressed with the teacher. The first question a principal should ask when a parent calls is, "Have you talked to the teacher?" Teachers can encourage principals to follow this process by saying something like, "Gee, I sure wish the parent had just talked to me first. It would have saved a lot of time and effort on your part."

If the issue remains unresolved, it's okay for concerned and/or dissatisfied parents to move on to the next level and the next and the next, up to and including the Board of Education or even the Commissioner or State School Board. It can be both costly and time consuming to move up the system, but some parents are willing to do it and sometimes it is absolutely the right thing to do.

Other times, it's stupid. But, hey, we can't control that.

It's both interesting and annoying that parents sometimes are disrespectful to the professional entrusted with their most prized possession—their child. Would any parent dream of talking to another professional the way some parents talk to teachers? Imagine a conversation like this:

Parent to minister: Reverend Hightower, my daughter should have the right to wear whatever she wants to church on Sunday.

The first question a principal should ask when a parent calls is, "Have you talked to the teacher?"

Or how about:

Parent to mechanic: You're not treating my car like
you do all the other cars.

Or maybe:

Parent to pediatrician: None of my son's friends have
to take an antibiotic. I think you're singling him out.

*Focus on
the 98% of
parents who
are supportive
and reasonable,
and develop the
skills you need
to withstand
the other 2%.*

Unlike some professionals, teachers generally do not have the
benefit of selecting their clientele. With practice, though, teachers
can develop their skills in interacting with parents so that, in the
end, the child benefits. As a teacher, you may not have picked the
child's parents to deal with, but neither did the child.

Focus on the 98% of parents who are supportive and reasonable,
and develop the skills you need to withstand the other 2%. With a
little practice, even the 2% can be tolerable if you keep your sense of
humor. If you follow some of the suggestions we've talked about,
someday you may even have this conversation:

Parent: I want to apologize for my behavior the other
day. I was upset. You were right about what my son
needs to do to be successful, and I will see that he
does it.

Teacher: Thank you. I appreciate your apology.

Parent: To show how sorry I am, I'm going to pay off
your college loans and start a campaign to increase
teachers' salaries by 50%.

Ha ha. Just a little joke. What the parent really says is this:

Parent: But I still think he deserved an A!

A FINAL ASSESSMENT

As we've pointed out earlier, this is the Age of Assessment—a test for everything. See how well you do in picking out the teacher's correct conversational responses in the following situations.

Item #1

> **Parent:** I know that on Flag Day all of the children get little flags. The kids gather at the flag pole in front of the school to sing the national anthem.
>
> **Teacher:** That's right. We've been doing it for years.
>
> **Parent:** Well, I think it's a waste of time. I want my child in class.
>
> **Teacher:** There isn't any "class" as such during that time. All the children will be outside.
>
> **Parent:** They should all be in class. My kid and everyone else's.

What should the teacher say next?

A. No problem. We'll just cancel Flag Day.

B. You sound pretty un-American to me.

C. Why don't you just keep your child home that day?

D. The Flag Day ceremony is part of our citizenship curriculum. If you have religious or philosophical
objections to the activity, your child can stay inside
and read in the library during that time.

Answer: *D.* But what if the parent says, "I don't want my child
excluded from any activities that all the other kids are going to do"?
Then what do you say?

A. Look, man, you can't have it both ways.

B. I appreciate your concerns, but those are really the
only choices.

C. Perhaps you should talk to our principal.

Right. Think A, say B, and be ready to move on to C.

Item #2

Parent: We're leaving for vacation three days early and
coming back three days late. Will Tanya miss anything?

What's the best response?

A. Nope. Nothing. We're just going to hang out for
those six days until she gets back.

B. Wait. Let me get this straight. You're taking your
child out of school for SIX DAYS and you're wondering if she'll miss anything?

C. We'll be introducing a new unit in geometry. We'll
be starting a new novel. And we'll be working on our
science research projects.

Answer: C. The reason you will not respond with either A or B is that you remember the basic rule: no sarcasm. Instead, you will respond professionally with C. Of course, you know what's coming next:

Parent: Oh, okay. So could you get Tanya's work ready for her in advance so she won't get behind?

What's your response this time?

A. When pigs fly.
B. I'll do my best, but I may not be able to have all the materials ready that far in advance.
C. Just tell her to take a book along to read.

Answer: B. We have already talked about why you won't respond with A. And while C is tempting, it gives the impression that Tanya really isn't going to miss anything important during the six days of class she will be gone. Despite your annoyance, do the best you can—and maybe add that she should take along a book to read anyway.

Item #3

Teacher: It appears that Drew took Cate's calculator from her desk.
Parent: What proof do you have?
Teacher: Cate reported it missing. So when the students went to art class, I checked all the desks. I found the calculator in Drew's desk.
Parent: Cate probably put it there just to get Drew in trouble.
Teacher: Actually, Drew admits he took the calculator.
Parent: You talked to my son without my being present? You had no right to do that!

Teacher: We do have a right to talk to our students.

Parent: Not without the parent present.

Teacher: The issue is that Drew took the calculator. He
has returned it to Cate, but I need you to talk to
Drew about respecting other people's property.

Parent: You had no right to talk to my son without me
being present!

Where should the teacher go from here?

A. We can't do anything about what's happened, but in
the future, I'll call you before I speak to Drew.

B. Can I count on you to talk to Drew?

C. For these kinds of incidents, the teacher does have
the responsibility to talk to the child. I will always
let you know, however, when there is a serious
problem.

Answer: Do not promise the parent you will call her every time
Drew runs into trouble. It's not practical, and you will not be able to
call every parent every time you need to speak to a student. Instead,
start with B. Remember the broken record technique? If this conversation continues, the teacher needs to keep her focus on the child's
behavior, not on whether the parent was present for the teacher's
conversation with her son. You will probably need to use answer C as
well, if the conversation continues.

Item #4

Parent: I hope you don't mind, but I brought you a
little present.

Teacher: A present? Why?

Parent: You've been so kind to Jessica.

Teacher: Jessica is a good student. She's easy to teach.

Parent: Well, just to show our appreciation, we'd like you to have this gift certificate for one of the clothing stores downtown.

Teacher: (*opening the envelope*) It's for $200!

Parent: It's the least we can do for all you've done for Jessica. And I know she'll be asking you for a college reference pretty soon too.

What is the teacher's next response?

A. Really, I can't accept this.

B. Jessica is a great student. I'd be happy to write her a reference. You don't have to give me anything to do it. I just can't accept this.

C. Actually, could you exchange this for a certificate for the hardware store? We need a new water heater.

Answer: Don't even think about C. Okay, maybe think about it while you're taking a cold shower at home. The first thing you say is A, followed immediately by B. Never accept a gift worth more than a couple of dollars from a parent. While some school districts prohibit gifts of any kind, most will allow the occasional coffee mug or plate of cookies at the holiday season. Never, ever accept a gift of alcohol (a nice bottle of wine, for example) or cash. Acceptance of such gifts compromises you and the profession.

Item #5

Parent: I'd like you to move Melissa's seat.

Teacher: Why?

Parent: I don't want her to have to sit next to that Williams kid.

Teacher: Why not?

Parent: Melissa came home with head lice last month.

Teacher: I remember that. We had several cases of it.

Parent: I'm sure the Williams kid gave them to her.

Teacher: I'm not sure the school nurse determined that.

Parent: Well, you know that boy's home life. His mother doesn't take care of those kids and everyone knows about the parties that go on in that house. The place is filthy. My daughter shouldn't have to be subjected to that kind of thing.

Teacher: Sitting next to Adam Williams doesn't subject Melissa to anything like that.

Parent: I want her moved. I don't want her coming home with head lice again from that boy.

What is the best response at this point?

A. Look on the bright side: If your daughter has head lice it means she has friends.

B. I don't talk about other children or their families.

C. I have a new seating arrangement every few weeks so that kids can learn to work with lots of children.

D. I'll move Melissa.

Answer: Here's why you can't choose D: If you do, you tacitly admit that "the Williams kid" gave Melissa head lice. If Melissa shouldn't sit next to him, then neither should anyone else.

As most elementary teachers know, once you have a contagious illness or infection (or infestation) in class, it's pretty hard to determine where it started. The important thing is to alert parents immediately to its presence and have the school nurse determine when infected children may safely return to school. Even if you suspect that the parent is correct about which child brought the head lice (or anything else) to class, your job is to share that information with the school nurse so that she can do a periodic check on that child. "The Williams kid" has enough problems without being ostracized by his classmates.

The first correct answer is B. Remember, you respect confidentiality and don't talk to parents about other children and their families.

What about A? It's only funny if your child is not infected.

Item #6

Parent: Rick needs to get at least a C in your class to be academically eligible to wrestle.

Teacher: He can pass this course if he does the homework.

Parent: It's tough for him. He has practice every night and he's tired when he gets home.

Teacher: He needs to do the homework so he can pass the tests.

Parent: Look, he has a good chance of getting a wrestling scholarship. He needs to stay eligible.

Which response from the teacher has the best chance of getting the parent's support?

A. All he has to do is do his homework.
B. Is he going to wrestle for a living when he gets out of college?
C. It's up to him if he wants to pass this course.
D. Look, I want him to stay eligible too. I want him to get a scholarship. How can we work together so that he gets his assignments done and he doesn't jeopardize his athletics?

Answer: Well, of course, the answer is *D*. Remember when we talked about pulling the parent over to your side? The first thing you have to do is acknowledge the parent's concerns and make it clear that you both want the same thing for the child—success.

But what if you answer *D* and the parent says, "You can make it work by not requiring so much homework"? You'll need to say something like this:

Teacher: I only require what is necessary for students to
pass the course. I will work with your son during
class and after school, but he needs to commit to
passing this course.

It's the best you can do.

Item #7

Parent: Why does John have to do this assignment
over?
Teacher: The assignment was to write an original story.
Parent: So?
Teacher: So John retold an episode of Star Trek.
Parent: That's impossible.
Teacher: Well, he changed the names, of course –
Captain Kirk becomes Captain Dirk, Spock becomes
Sprok—that sort of thing—but it's still a Star Trek
episode.
Parent: I'd like to see proof of that. You haven't seen
every Star Trek episode. How would you know?
Teacher: Well, you're right. I haven't seen them all.
But as luck would have it, this happens to be one I
have seen.

Parent: My son isn't writing anything over until I have
proof. John, is this your work?

John: Yes, it is.

Parent: If he says it is, then it is. My son doesn't lie.

Unless the teacher knows Klingon, which would put an immediate
end to the discussion, he'll have to choose from one of these responses:

A. I'm sorry we don't agree on this, but I'm going to
insist that John redo the assignment and write an
original story.

B. Okay, I'll see if I can go back through all the
episodes of Star Trek until I can find it and prove
to you.

C. All kids lie at some point. Even yours.

Answer: I'm sure you realize that even if you think C is true,
saying it will only inflame the situation. B is a poor choice because
even if you had the time and energy to find the exact episode that
was used, the parent still may not believe there is enough similarity to
prove anything. Go with A. If the parent says, "Well, John isn't
going to do it," you know what the next response is.

Teacher: Then he will get a zero for the assignment.

And you know what to say when the parent says, "I'm going to
see the principal."

Teacher: You need to do what you think is right.

Item #8

Teacher: Michael has lost his computer privileges
because once again I found him at a site that is not
appropriate for students.

Parent: Frankly, I have a problem with that.

Teacher: I'm glad to hear that. We can't block everything on our server, and sometimes students can get
to places they shouldn't be.

Parent: No, you misunderstood. I have a problem with
Mike losing his privileges.

Teacher: Mike was warned twice about accessing
pornography sites. The third time he loses his
privileges for a week.

Parent: He says he got there by accident.

Teacher: I checked the history of where he'd been.
That was no accident.

Parent: Well, he's a normal boy. But even so, it's your
responsibility to watch how kids use the computers.

Teacher: Exactly. And I do. That's why he's off the
computer for a week.

Parent: So how is he supposed to get his work done?

What is the best response at this point?

A. What do I care? This is his third offense!

B. He will have to work the old fashioned way – writing
by hand and researching in the library.

C. He'll have to figure that out, I guess.

Answer: *B,* of course. What a hardship! How awful! How will
he ever do it? Second Answer: Just like every teacher over 40 did when
he or she was in middle school.

Item #8

Teacher: Glad you were able to come to the conference,
Mr. Berman.

Parent: Call me Fred.

Teacher: Okay, Fred. Your daughter is failing history.

Parent: Call me Mr. Berman.

Teacher: Well, Mr. Berman, your daughter is still failing history.

Parent: Does she need it to graduate?

Teacher: Yes, she does.

Parent: Well, Nanette, I think you have your work cut out.

Which is the teacher's best reply?

A. Well, Fred, hang on to those graduation announcements.

B. Well, Fred, I think your daughter has her work cut out.

C. Well, Fred, I'm going to need your help.

Answer: Remember that we prefer that both teacher and parent use the appropriate respective titles, but if the parent uses your first name, you can use his. Otherwise it's an uneven playing field. The answer is C.

Item #9

Parent: I'm sick and tired of your picking on my daughter.

Teacher: I'm not picking on her. But I cannot tolerate her disrespect.

Parent: She says you don't respect her.

Teacher: I respect all my students. But I will not tolerate your daughter's language.

Parent: You know you don't like her. Other kids do the same thing and you just pick on her.

Teacher: Other kids do not use that language in my
class.

Parent: If you ever kick her out of class again, you're
going to answer to me!

What is the best response?

A. This conference is over.

Answer: A.

I'm sure you did very well on the assessment. You know that
working with difficult parents requires practice, common sense, and
keeping your wits about you.

As you've probably realized by now, describing difficult parents as
"types" is simply a way to talk about specific strategies a teacher can
use in specific situations. Difficult parents are more alike than dis-
similar in their demands on the teacher and their refusal to allow
their child to take responsibility for his or her own actions. A
Helicopter can turn into a Caped Crusader overnight. The Stealth
Zapper can double as the Uncivil Libertarian. What's important is
not who's who, but what skills and strategies we've developed to deal
with difficult parents.

Good teaching is not easy. It never was. And it is likely that parents will become more, not less, demanding. Teachers need not only
to develop strategies to deal with parents, but also to develop a habit
of reflecting upon their own teaching behaviors to avoid unnecessary
conflicts.

Throughout this book you've seen dozens of examples of conversations with parents that go downhill fast. Let's end with a couple of
examples that show how parents and teachers can work together for
the good of the child.

Here's one conversation that puts the child's best interests first:

Teacher: Rob is a really bright kid. He needs to put more effort into his work.

Parent: I think sometimes because things are easy for him, he doesn't feel he has to try as hard.

Teacher: You could be right. I'm thinking about putting together a small group of kids to read a more challenging book this semester. What do you think?

Parent: I think he'd love it.

Here's another example:

Teacher: It appears that Emma copied Larry's work on this assignment.

Parent: Really? How do you know?

Teacher: Well, the papers were similar. I talked with both kids, and Emma admitted that she copied his work.

Parent: Did you talk to her?

Teacher: Yes, I did. She was very embarrassed.

Parent: Well, she should be. We'll have a discussion when we get home.

Teacher: I do have some concern that she said she just doesn't have time to get everything done with basketball, dance lessons, and flute lessons.

Parent: Maybe we need to look at her schedule. Her schoolwork is the most important thing.

When parents and teachers are partners, it's wonderful for the child—and it's pretty terrific for the parents and teachers too!

Suzanne Capek Tingley has been a teacher and principal and is currently a school superintendent. She teaches education administration as an adjunct for the State University of New York at Oswego. Her work has appeared in *Education Week, The School Administrator, Educational Leadership,* and other publications. Among her awards is Outstanding School Administrator from the New York State Association of Library Media Specialists.